THIS JOURNAL BELONGS TO:

_____

_____

BOOK INDEX

Page	Title	Author
1		
2		
3		
4		
5		
6		
7		
8		
9		
10		
11		
12		
13		
14		
15		
16		
17		
18		
19		
20		
21		
22		
23		
24		
25		

BOOK INDEX

Page	Title	Author
26		
27		
28		
29		
30		
31		
32		
33		
34		
35		
36		
37		
38		
39		
40		
41		
42		
43		
44		
45		
46		
47		
48		
49		
50		

BOOK INDEX

Page	Title	Author
51		
52		
53		
54		
55		
56		
57		
58		
59		
60		
61		
62		
63		
64		
65		
66		
67		
68		
69		
70		
71		
72		
73		
74		
75		

BOOK INDEX

Page	Title	Author
76		
77		
78		
79		
80		
81		
82		
83		
84		
85		
86		
87		
88		
89		
90		
91		
92		
93		
94		
95		
96		
97		
98		
99		
100		

 **TITLE:**

Author: _____ *Publisher:* _____

FORMAT: ○ *Hardcover* ○ *Paperback* ○ *Ebook* ○ *Audiobook*
CATEGORY: ○ *Fiction* ○ *Non-fiction* *Genre/Subject:* _____
SOURCE: ○ *Bought* ○ *Borrowed* ○ *Received from:* _____

Page Count: _____
Date Started: _____
Date Finished: _____

📖 *WHY I CHOSE THIS BOOK:*
_____
_____

👑 *FAVORITE PART:*
(draw or describe)

✒ *NOTES/REVIEW:*
_____
_____
_____
_____
_____
_____
_____
_____
_____
_____
_____
_____
_____
_____
_____
_____
_____
_____

FICTION	NON-FICTION
Ease of Reading:	*Ease of Reading:*
☆☆☆☆☆	☆☆☆☆☆
Characters:	*Substantiality:*
☆☆☆☆☆	☆☆☆☆☆
Plot:	*Impactfulness:*
☆☆☆☆☆	☆☆☆☆☆

Overall Rating: ☆☆☆☆☆

🎖 *RECOMMEND?* ○ *Yes* ○ *No*

💡 *QUOTES/REFLECTIONS/EPIPHANIES:*
_____
_____
_____
_____
_____
_____
_____
_____

TITLE:

Author: _____ Publisher: _____

FORMAT: ○ Hardcover   ○ Paperback   ○ Ebook   ○ Audiobook
CATEGORY: ○ Fiction ○ Non-fiction Genre/Subject: _____
SOURCE: ○ Bought ○ Borrowed ○ Received from: _____

Page Count: _____
Date Started: _____
Date Finished: _____

📖 WHY I CHOSE THIS BOOK:
_____
_____

♛ FAVORITE PART:
(draw or describe)

✒ NOTES/REVIEW:
_____
_____
_____
_____
_____
_____
_____
_____
_____
_____
_____
_____
_____
_____
_____
_____
_____

FICTION	NON-FICTION
Ease of Reading: ☆☆☆☆☆	Ease of Reading: ☆☆☆☆☆
Characters: ☆☆☆☆☆	Substantiality: ☆☆☆☆☆
Plot: ☆☆☆☆☆	Impactfulness: ☆☆☆☆☆

Overall Rating: ☆☆☆☆☆

🏅 RECOMMEND?   ○ Yes   ○ No

💡 QUOTES/REFLECTIONS/EPIPHANIES:
_____
_____
_____
_____
_____
_____
_____
_____

📚 **TITLE:**

Author: _____ *Publisher:* _____

FORMAT: ○ *Hardcover* ○ *Paperback* ○ *Ebook* ○ *Audiobook*
CATEGORY: ○ *Fiction* ○ *Non-fiction* *Genre/Subject:* _____
SOURCE: ○ *Bought* ○ *Borrowed* ○ *Received from:* _____

Page Count: _____
Date Started: _____
Date Finished: _____

📖 *WHY I CHOSE THIS BOOK:*
_____
_____

👑 *FAVORITE PART:*
(draw or describe)

✒ *NOTES/REVIEW:*
_____
_____
_____
_____
_____
_____
_____
_____
_____
_____
_____
_____
_____
_____
_____
_____

FICTION	NON-FICTION
Ease of Reading:	Ease of Reading:
☆☆☆☆☆	☆☆☆☆☆
Characters:	Substantiality:
☆☆☆☆☆	☆☆☆☆☆
Plot:	Impactfulness:
☆☆☆☆☆	☆☆☆☆☆

Overall Rating: ☆☆☆☆☆

🏅 *RECOMMEND?* ○ *Yes* ○ *No*

💡 *QUOTES/REFLECTIONS/EPIPHANIES:*
_____
_____
_____
_____
_____
_____
_____

TITLE:

Author: _____ Publisher: _____

FORMAT: ○ Hardcover ○ Paperback ○ Ebook ○ Audiobook
CATEGORY: ○ Fiction ○ Non-fiction Genre/Subject: _____
SOURCE: ○ Bought ○ Borrowed ○ Received from: _____

Page Count: _____
Date Started: _____
Date Finished: _____

WHY I CHOSE THIS BOOK:
_____
_____

FAVORITE PART:
(draw or describe)

NOTES/REVIEW:
_____
_____
_____
_____
_____
_____
_____
_____
_____
_____
_____
_____
_____
_____
_____
_____
_____
_____

FICTION	NON-FICTION
Ease of Reading: ☆☆☆☆☆	Ease of Reading: ☆☆☆☆☆
Characters: ☆☆☆☆☆	Substantiality: ☆☆☆☆☆
Plot: ☆☆☆☆☆	Impactfulness: ☆☆☆☆☆

Overall Rating: ☆☆☆☆☆

RECOMMEND? ○ Yes ○ No

QUOTES/REFLECTIONS/EPIPHANIES:
_____
_____
_____
_____
_____
_____
_____
_____
_____

TITLE:

Author: _____ *Publisher:* _____

FORMAT: ○ *Hardcover* ○ *Paperback* ○ *Ebook* ○ *Audiobook*
CATEGORY: ○ *Fiction* ○ *Non-fiction* *Genre/Subject:* _____
SOURCE: ○ *Bought* ○ *Borrowed* ○ *Received from:* _____

Page Count: _____
Date Started: _____
Date Finished: _____

WHY I CHOSE THIS BOOK:
_____
_____

FAVORITE PART:
(draw or describe)

NOTES/REVIEW:
_____
_____
_____
_____
_____
_____
_____
_____
_____
_____
_____
_____
_____
_____
_____
_____
_____
_____

FICTION	NON-FICTION
Ease of Reading:	Ease of Reading:
☆☆☆☆☆	☆☆☆☆☆
Characters:	Substantiality:
☆☆☆☆☆	☆☆☆☆☆
Plot:	Impactfulness:
☆☆☆☆☆	☆☆☆☆☆

Overall Rating: ☆☆☆☆☆

RECOMMEND? ○ *Yes* ○ *No*

QUOTES/REFLECTIONS/EPIPHANIES:
_____
_____
_____
_____
_____
_____
_____
_____
_____

TITLE:

Author: _____ Publisher: _____

FORMAT: ○ Hardcover ○ Paperback ○ Ebook ○ Audiobook
CATEGORY: ○ Fiction ○ Non-fiction Genre/Subject: _____
SOURCE: ○ Bought ○ Borrowed ○ Received from: _____

Page Count: _____
Date Started: _____
Date Finished: _____

WHY I CHOSE THIS BOOK:
_____
_____
_____

♔ FAVORITE PART:
(draw or describe)

✐ NOTES/REVIEW:

	FICTION	NON-FICTION
Ease of Reading:	☆☆☆☆☆	☆☆☆☆☆
Characters:	☆☆☆☆☆	Substantiality: ☆☆☆☆☆
Plot:	☆☆☆☆☆	Impactfulness: ☆☆☆☆☆

Overall Rating: ☆☆☆☆☆

♖ RECOMMEND? ○ Yes ○ No

💡 QUOTES/REFLECTIONS/EPIPHANIES:

TITLE:

Author: _____ *Publisher:* _____

FORMAT: ○ *Hardcover* ○ *Paperback* ○ *Ebook* ○ *Audiobook*
CATEGORY: ○ *Fiction* ○ *Non-fiction* *Genre/Subject:* _____
SOURCE: ○ *Bought* ○ *Borrowed* ○ *Received from:* _____

Page Count: _____
Date Started: _____
Date Finished: _____

WHY I CHOSE THIS BOOK:
_____
_____

♕ FAVORITE PART:
(draw or describe)

✎ NOTES/REVIEW:

FICTION	NON-FICTION
Ease of Reading:	*Ease of Reading:*
☆☆☆☆☆	☆☆☆☆☆
Characters:	*Substantiality:*
☆☆☆☆☆	☆☆☆☆☆
Plot:	*Impactfulness:*
☆☆☆☆☆	☆☆☆☆☆

Overall Rating: ☆☆☆☆☆

⚇ RECOMMEND? ○ *Yes* ○ *No*

QUOTES/REFLECTIONS/EPIPHANIES:
_____
_____
_____
_____
_____
_____
_____

TITLE: _____

Author: _____ Publisher: _____

FORMAT: ○ Hardcover   ○ Paperback   ○ Ebook   ○ Audiobook
CATEGORY: ○ Fiction ○ Non-fiction   Genre/Subject: _____
SOURCE: ○ Bought ○ Borrowed ○ Received from: _____

Page Count: _____
Date Started: _____
Date Finished: _____

WHY I CHOSE THIS BOOK:
_____
_____

♔ FAVORITE PART:
(draw or describe)

✎ NOTES/REVIEW:
_____
_____
_____
_____
_____
_____
_____
_____
_____
_____
_____
_____
_____
_____
_____
_____

FICTION	NON-FICTION
Ease of Reading:	Ease of Reading:
☆☆☆☆☆	☆☆☆☆☆
Characters:	Substantiality:
☆☆☆☆☆	☆☆☆☆☆
Plot:	Impactfulness:
☆☆☆☆☆	☆☆☆☆☆

Overall Rating: ☆☆☆☆☆

⚔ RECOMMEND?   ○ Yes   ○ No

💡 QUOTES/REFLECTIONS/EPIPHANIES:
_____
_____
_____
_____
_____
_____
_____
_____
_____

TITLE:

Author: _____ *Publisher:* _____

FORMAT: ○ *Hardcover* ○ *Paperback* ○ *Ebook* ○ *Audiobook*
CATEGORY: ○ *Fiction* ○ *Non-fiction* *Genre/Subject:* _____
SOURCE: ○ *Bought* ○ *Borrowed* ○ *Received from:* _____

Page Count: _____
Date Started: _____
Date Finished: _____

WHY I CHOSE THIS BOOK:
_____
_____

♔ *FAVORITE PART:*
(draw or describe)

✍ *NOTES/REVIEW:*
_____
_____
_____
_____
_____
_____
_____
_____
_____
_____
_____
_____
_____
_____
_____
_____
_____

FICTION	NON-FICTION
Ease of Reading:	Ease of Reading:
☆☆☆☆☆	☆☆☆☆☆
Characters:	Substantiality:
☆☆☆☆☆	☆☆☆☆☆
Plot:	Impactfulness:
☆☆☆☆☆	☆☆☆☆☆

Overall Rating: ☆☆☆☆☆

⚜ *RECOMMEND?* ○ *Yes* ○ *No*

💡 *QUOTES/REFLECTIONS/EPIPHANIES:*
_____
_____
_____
_____
_____
_____
_____
_____

TITLE:

Author: _____ Publisher: _____

FORMAT: ○ Hardcover   ○ Paperback   ○ Ebook   ○ Audiobook
CATEGORY: ○ Fiction ○ Non-fiction   Genre/Subject: _____
SOURCE: ○ Bought ○ Borrowed ○ Received from: _____

Page Count: _____
Date Started: _____
Date Finished: _____

WHY I CHOSE THIS BOOK:
_____
_____

♛ FAVORITE PART:
(draw or describe)

✎ NOTES/REVIEW:
_____
_____
_____
_____
_____
_____
_____
_____
_____
_____
_____
_____
_____
_____
_____

FICTION	NON-FICTION
Ease of Reading:	Ease of Reading:
☆☆☆☆☆	☆☆☆☆☆
Characters:	Substantiality:
☆☆☆☆☆	☆☆☆☆☆
Plot:	Impactfulness:
☆☆☆☆☆	☆☆☆☆☆

Overall Rating: ☆☆☆☆☆

⚜ RECOMMEND?   ○ Yes   ○ No

💡 QUOTES/REFLECTIONS/EPIPHANIES:
_____
_____
_____
_____
_____
_____
_____
_____

TITLE:

Author: _____ *Publisher:* _____

FORMAT: ○ *Hardcover*   ○ *Paperback*   ○ *Ebook*   ○ *Audiobook*
CATEGORY: ○ *Fiction* ○ *Non-fiction*   *Genre/Subject:* _____
SOURCE: ○ *Bought* ○ *Borrowed* ○ *Received from:* _____

Page Count: _____
Date Started: _____
Date Finished: _____

WHY I CHOSE THIS BOOK:
_____
_____

♕ FAVORITE PART:
(draw or describe)

✎ NOTES/REVIEW:
_____
_____
_____
_____
_____
_____
_____
_____
_____
_____
_____
_____
_____
_____
_____
_____
_____
_____

FICTION	NON-FICTION
Ease of Reading:	*Ease of Reading:*
☆☆☆☆☆	☆☆☆☆☆
Characters:	*Substantiality:*
☆☆☆☆☆	☆☆☆☆☆
Plot:	*Impactfulness:*
☆☆☆☆☆	☆☆☆☆☆

Overall Rating: ☆☆☆☆☆

♖ RECOMMEND? ○ *Yes* ○ *No*

QUOTES/REFLECTIONS/EPIPHANIES:
_____
_____
_____
_____
_____
_____
_____
_____

TITLE:

Author: _____ Publisher: _____

FORMAT: ○ Hardcover ○ Paperback ○ Ebook ○ Audiobook
CATEGORY: ○ Fiction ○ Non-fiction Genre/Subject: _____
SOURCE: ○ Bought ○ Borrowed ○ Received from: _____

Page Count: _____
Date Started: _____
Date Finished: _____

WHY I CHOSE THIS BOOK:
_____
_____

♛ FAVORITE PART:
(draw or describe)

✒ NOTES/REVIEW:
_____
_____
_____
_____
_____
_____
_____
_____
_____
_____
_____
_____
_____
_____
_____

FICTION	NON-FICTION
Ease of Reading: ☆☆☆☆☆	Ease of Reading: ☆☆☆☆☆
Characters: ☆☆☆☆☆	Substantiality: ☆☆☆☆☆
Plot: ☆☆☆☆☆	Impactfulness: ☆☆☆☆☆

Overall Rating: ☆☆☆☆☆

⚜ RECOMMEND? ○ Yes ○ No

💡 QUOTES/REFLECTIONS/EPIPHANIES:
_____
_____
_____
_____
_____
_____
_____
_____

TITLE:

Author: _____ *Publisher:* _____

FORMAT: ○ *Hardcover* ○ *Paperback* ○ *Ebook* ○ *Audiobook*
CATEGORY: ○ *Fiction* ○ *Non-fiction* *Genre/Subject:* _____
SOURCE: ○ *Bought* ○ *Borrowed* ○ *Received from:* _____

Page Count: _____
Date Started: _____
Date Finished: _____

WHY I CHOSE THIS BOOK:
_____
_____

FAVORITE PART:
(draw or describe)

NOTES/REVIEW:
_____
_____
_____
_____
_____
_____
_____
_____
_____
_____
_____
_____
_____
_____
_____
_____
_____
_____

FICTION	NON-FICTION
Ease of Reading:	Ease of Reading:
☆☆☆☆☆	☆☆☆☆☆
Characters:	Substantiality:
☆☆☆☆☆	☆☆☆☆☆
Plot:	Impactfulness:
☆☆☆☆☆	☆☆☆☆☆

Overall Rating: ☆☆☆☆☆

RECOMMEND? ○ *Yes* ○ *No*

QUOTES/REFLECTIONS/EPIPHANIES:
_____
_____
_____
_____
_____
_____
_____
_____

TITLE:

Author: _____ Publisher: _____

FORMAT: ○ Hardcover ○ Paperback ○ Ebook ○ Audiobook
CATEGORY: ○ Fiction ○ Non-fiction Genre/Subject: _____
SOURCE: ○ Bought ○ Borrowed ○ Received from: _____

Page Count: _____
Date Started: _____
Date Finished: _____

WHY I CHOSE THIS BOOK:
_____
_____

♛ FAVORITE PART:
(draw or describe)

✎ NOTES/REVIEW:
_____
_____
_____
_____
_____
_____
_____
_____
_____
_____
_____
_____
_____
_____
_____
_____
_____

FICTION	NON-FICTION
Ease of Reading:	Ease of Reading:
☆☆☆☆☆	☆☆☆☆☆
Characters:	Substantiality:
☆☆☆☆☆	☆☆☆☆☆
Plot:	Impactfulness:
☆☆☆☆☆	☆☆☆☆☆

Overall Rating: ☆☆☆☆☆

✿ RECOMMEND? ○ Yes ○ No

💡 QUOTES/REFLECTIONS/EPIPHANIES:
_____
_____
_____
_____
_____
_____
_____
_____

TITLE:

Author: _____ Publisher: _____

FORMAT: ○ Hardcover ○ Paperback ○ Ebook ○ Audiobook
CATEGORY: ○ Fiction ○ Non-fiction Genre/Subject: _____
SOURCE: ○ Bought ○ Borrowed ○ Received from: _____

Page Count: _____
Date Started: _____
Date Finished: _____

📖 WHY I CHOSE THIS BOOK:
_____
_____

♛ FAVORITE PART:
(draw or describe)

🖋 NOTES/REVIEW:

FICTION	NON-FICTION
Ease of Reading:	Ease of Reading:
☆☆☆☆☆	☆☆☆☆☆
Characters:	Substantiality:
☆☆☆☆☆	☆☆☆☆☆
Plot:	Impactfulness:
☆☆☆☆☆	☆☆☆☆☆

Overall Rating: ☆☆☆☆☆

🏅 RECOMMEND? ○ Yes ○ No

💡 QUOTES/REFLECTIONS/EPIPHANIES:
_____
_____
_____
_____
_____
_____
_____

TITLE:

Author: _____ Publisher: _____

FORMAT: ○ Hardcover　○ Paperback　○ Ebook　○ Audiobook
CATEGORY: ○ Fiction ○ Non-fiction　Genre/Subject: _____
SOURCE: ○ Bought ○ Borrowed ○ Received from: _____

Page Count: _____
Date Started: _____
Date Finished: _____

📖 WHY I CHOSE THIS BOOK:
_____
_____

👑 FAVORITE PART:
(draw or describe)

✒ NOTES/REVIEW:
_____
_____
_____
_____
_____
_____
_____
_____
_____
_____
_____
_____
_____
_____
_____
_____

FICTION	NON-FICTION
Ease of Reading:	Ease of Reading:
☆☆☆☆☆	☆☆☆☆☆
Characters:	Substantiality:
☆☆☆☆☆	☆☆☆☆☆
Plot:	Impactfulness:
☆☆☆☆☆	☆☆☆☆☆

Overall Rating: ☆☆☆☆☆

🎖 RECOMMEND?　○ Yes　○ No

💡 QUOTES/REFLECTIONS/EPIPHANIES:
_____
_____
_____
_____
_____
_____
_____
_____

TITLE:

Author: _____ *Publisher:* _____

FORMAT: ○ *Hardcover* ○ *Paperback* ○ *Ebook* ○ *Audiobook*
CATEGORY: ○ *Fiction* ○ *Non-fiction* *Genre/Subject:* _____
SOURCE: ○ *Bought* ○ *Borrowed* ○ *Received from:* _____

Page Count: _____
Date Started: _____
Date Finished: _____

📖 *WHY I CHOSE THIS BOOK:*
_____
_____

👑 *FAVORITE PART:*
(draw or describe)

✒ *NOTES/REVIEW:*

	FICTION	NON-FICTION
Ease of Reading:	☆☆☆☆☆	☆☆☆☆☆
Characters: / Substantiality:	☆☆☆☆☆	☆☆☆☆☆
Plot: / Impactfulness:	☆☆☆☆☆	☆☆☆☆☆

Overall Rating: ☆☆☆☆☆

🏅 *RECOMMEND?* ○ *Yes* ○ *No*

💡 *QUOTES/REFLECTIONS/EPIPHANIES:*
_____
_____
_____
_____
_____
_____
_____
_____

📚 TITLE:

Author: _____ Publisher: _____

FORMAT: ○ Hardcover   ○ Paperback   ○ Ebook   ○ Audiobook
CATEGORY: ○ Fiction ○ Non-fiction   Genre/Subject: _____
SOURCE: ○ Bought ○ Borrowed ○ Received from: _____

Page Count: _____
Date Started: _____
Date Finished: _____

📖 WHY I CHOSE THIS BOOK:
_____
_____

👑 FAVORITE PART:
(draw or describe)

✒ NOTES/REVIEW:
_____
_____
_____
_____
_____
_____
_____
_____
_____
_____
_____
_____
_____
_____
_____
_____
_____

FICTION	NON-FICTION
Ease of Reading:	Ease of Reading:
☆☆☆☆☆	☆☆☆☆☆
Characters:	Substantiality:
☆☆☆☆☆	☆☆☆☆☆
Plot:	Impactfulness:
☆☆☆☆☆	☆☆☆☆☆

Overall Rating: ☆☆☆☆☆

🏅 RECOMMEND?   ○ Yes   ○ No

💡 QUOTES/REFLECTIONS/EPIPHANIES:
_____
_____
_____
_____
_____
_____
_____
_____

TITLE:

Author: _____   Publisher: _____

FORMAT: ○ Hardcover   ○ Paperback   ○ Ebook   ○ Audiobook
CATEGORY: ○ Fiction ○ Non-fiction   Genre/Subject: _____
SOURCE: ○ Bought ○ Borrowed ○ Received from: _____

Page Count: _____
Date Started: _____
Date Finished: _____

📖 WHY I CHOSE THIS BOOK:
_____
_____

👑 FAVORITE PART:
(draw or describe)

✒ NOTES/REVIEW:
_____
_____
_____
_____
_____
_____
_____
_____
_____
_____
_____
_____
_____
_____
_____
_____
_____

FICTION	NON-FICTION
Ease of Reading:	Ease of Reading:
☆☆☆☆☆	☆☆☆☆☆
Characters:	Substantiality:
☆☆☆☆☆	☆☆☆☆☆
Plot:	Impactfulness:
☆☆☆☆☆	☆☆☆☆☆

Overall Rating: ☆☆☆☆☆

🏅 RECOMMEND?   ○ Yes   ○ No

💡 QUOTES/REFLECTIONS/EPIPHANIES:
_____
_____
_____
_____
_____
_____
_____
_____

TITLE:

Author: _____ Publisher: _____

FORMAT: ○ Hardcover ○ Paperback ○ Ebook ○ Audiobook
CATEGORY: ○ Fiction ○ Non-fiction Genre/Subject: _____
SOURCE: ○ Bought ○ Borrowed ○ Received from: _____

Page Count: _____
Date Started: _____
Date Finished: _____

WHY I CHOSE THIS BOOK:
_____
_____

♔ FAVORITE PART:
(draw or describe)

✒ NOTES/REVIEW:
_____
_____
_____
_____
_____
_____
_____
_____
_____
_____
_____
_____
_____
_____
_____
_____
_____

FICTION	NON-FICTION
Ease of Reading:	Ease of Reading:
☆☆☆☆☆	☆☆☆☆☆
Characters:	Substantiality:
☆☆☆☆☆	☆☆☆☆☆
Plot:	Impactfulness:
☆☆☆☆☆	☆☆☆☆☆

Overall Rating: ☆☆☆☆☆

RECOMMEND? ○ Yes ○ No

QUOTES/REFLECTIONS/EPIPHANIES:
_____
_____
_____
_____
_____
_____
_____
_____

📚 **TITLE:**

Author: _____ *Publisher:* _____

FORMAT: ○ *Hardcover* ○ *Paperback* ○ *Ebook* ○ *Audiobook*
CATEGORY: ○ *Fiction* ○ *Non-fiction* *Genre/Subject:* _____
SOURCE: ○ *Bought* ○ *Borrowed* ○ *Received from:* _____

Page Count: _____
Date Started: _____
Date Finished: _____

📖 *WHY I CHOSE THIS BOOK:*
_____
_____

👑 *FAVORITE PART:*
(draw or describe)

🖋 *NOTES/REVIEW:*
_____
_____
_____
_____
_____
_____
_____
_____
_____
_____
_____
_____
_____
_____
_____
_____
_____
_____

FICTION	NON-FICTION
Ease of Reading:	Ease of Reading:
☆☆☆☆☆	☆☆☆☆☆
Characters:	Substantiality:
☆☆☆☆☆	☆☆☆☆☆
Plot:	Impactfulness:
☆☆☆☆☆	☆☆☆☆☆

Overall Rating: ☆☆☆☆☆

🏅 *RECOMMEND?* ○ *Yes* ○ *No*

💡 *QUOTES/REFLECTIONS/EPIPHANIES:*
_____
_____
_____
_____
_____
_____
_____
_____

TITLE:

Author: _____ Publisher: _____

FORMAT: ○ Hardcover   ○ Paperback   ○ Ebook   ○ Audiobook
CATEGORY: ○ Fiction ○ Non-fiction Genre/Subject: _____
SOURCE: ○ Bought ○ Borrowed ○ Received from: _____

Page Count: _____
Date Started: _____
Date Finished: _____

WHY I CHOSE THIS BOOK:
_____
_____

♔ FAVORITE PART:
(draw or describe)

✎ NOTES/REVIEW:
_____
_____
_____
_____
_____
_____
_____
_____
_____
_____
_____
_____
_____
_____
_____
_____
_____

FICTION	NON-FICTION
Ease of Reading: ☆☆☆☆☆	Ease of Reading: ☆☆☆☆☆
Characters: ☆☆☆☆☆	Substantiality: ☆☆☆☆☆
Plot: ☆☆☆☆☆	Impactfulness: ☆☆☆☆☆

Overall Rating: ☆☆☆☆☆

♛ RECOMMEND? ○ Yes ○ No

💡 QUOTES/REFLECTIONS/EPIPHANIES:
_____
_____
_____
_____
_____
_____
_____
_____

TITLE:

Author: _____ *Publisher:* _____

FORMAT: ○ *Hardcover*　　○ *Paperback*　　○ *Ebook*　　○ *Audiobook*
CATEGORY: ○ *Fiction* ○ *Non-fiction*　*Genre/Subject:* _____
SOURCE: ○ *Bought* ○ *Borrowed* ○ *Received from:* _____

Page Count: _____
Date Started: _____
Date Finished: _____

📖 *WHY I CHOSE THIS BOOK:*
_____
_____

👑 *FAVORITE PART:*
(draw or describe)

✒ *NOTES/REVIEW:*
_____
_____
_____
_____
_____
_____
_____
_____
_____
_____
_____
_____
_____
_____
_____
_____
_____

FICTION	NON-FICTION
Ease of Reading:	*Ease of Reading:*
☆☆☆☆☆	☆☆☆☆☆
Characters:	*Substantiality:*
☆☆☆☆☆	☆☆☆☆☆
Plot:	*Impactfulness:*
☆☆☆☆☆	☆☆☆☆☆

Overall Rating: ☆☆☆☆☆

🏅 *RECOMMEND?*　○ *Yes*　○ *No*

💡 *QUOTES/REFLECTIONS/EPIPHANIES:*
_____
_____
_____
_____
_____
_____
_____
_____

TITLE:

Author: _____ Publisher: _____

FORMAT: ○ Hardcover   ○ Paperback   ○ Ebook   ○ Audiobook
CATEGORY: ○ Fiction ○ Non-fiction   Genre/Subject: _____
SOURCE: ○ Bought ○ Borrowed ○ Received from: _____

Page Count: _____
Date Started: _____
Date Finished: _____

WHY I CHOSE THIS BOOK:
_____
_____

FAVORITE PART:
(draw or describe)

NOTES/REVIEW:
_____
_____
_____
_____
_____
_____
_____
_____
_____
_____
_____
_____
_____
_____
_____
_____

FICTION	NON-FICTION
Ease of Reading: ☆☆☆☆☆	Ease of Reading: ☆☆☆☆☆
Characters: ☆☆☆☆☆	Substantiality: ☆☆☆☆☆
Plot: ☆☆☆☆☆	Impactfulness: ☆☆☆☆☆

Overall Rating: ☆☆☆☆☆

RECOMMEND?   ○ Yes   ○ No

QUOTES/REFLECTIONS/EPIPHANIES:
_____
_____
_____
_____
_____
_____
_____
_____

📚 TITLE:

Author: _____ *Publisher:* _____

FORMAT: ○ *Hardcover* ○ *Paperback* ○ *Ebook* ○ *Audiobook*
CATEGORY: ○ *Fiction* ○ *Non-fiction* *Genre/Subject:* _____
SOURCE: ○ *Bought* ○ *Borrowed* ○ *Received from:* _____

Page Count: _____
Date Started: _____
Date Finished: _____

📖 *WHY I CHOSE THIS BOOK:*
_____
_____

👑 *FAVORITE PART:*
(draw or describe)

🖊 *NOTES/REVIEW:*
_____
_____
_____
_____
_____
_____
_____
_____
_____
_____
_____
_____
_____
_____
_____
_____
_____

FICTION	NON-FICTION
Ease of Reading:	Ease of Reading:
☆☆☆☆☆	☆☆☆☆☆
Characters:	Substantiality:
☆☆☆☆☆	☆☆☆☆☆
Plot:	Impactfulness:
☆☆☆☆☆	☆☆☆☆☆

Overall Rating: ☆☆☆☆☆

🏅 *RECOMMEND?* ○ *Yes* ○ *No*

💡 *QUOTES/REFLECTIONS/EPIPHANIES:*
_____
_____
_____
_____
_____
_____
_____
_____

📚 TITLE:

Author: _____ Publisher: _____

FORMAT: ○ Hardcover ○ Paperback ○ Ebook ○ Audiobook
CATEGORY: ○ Fiction ○ Non-fiction Genre/Subject: _____
SOURCE: ○ Bought ○ Borrowed ○ Received from: _____

Page Count: _____
Date Started: _____
Date Finished: _____

📖 WHY I CHOSE THIS BOOK:
_____
_____

👑 FAVORITE PART:
(draw or describe)

✍ NOTES/REVIEW:
_____
_____
_____
_____
_____
_____
_____
_____
_____
_____
_____
_____
_____
_____
_____
_____

FICTION	NON-FICTION
Ease of Reading:	Ease of Reading:
☆☆☆☆☆	☆☆☆☆☆
Characters:	Substantiality:
☆☆☆☆☆	☆☆☆☆☆
Plot:	Impactfulness:
☆☆☆☆☆	☆☆☆☆☆

Overall Rating: ☆☆☆☆☆

🎗 RECOMMEND? ○ Yes ○ No

💡 QUOTES/REFLECTIONS/EPIPHANIES:
_____
_____
_____
_____
_____
_____
_____
_____

📚 **TITLE:**

Author: _____ *Publisher:* _____

FORMAT: ○ *Hardcover* ○ *Paperback* ○ *Ebook* ○ *Audiobook*
CATEGORY: ○ *Fiction* ○ *Non-fiction* *Genre/Subject:* _____
SOURCE: ○ *Bought* ○ *Borrowed* ○ *Received from:* _____

Page Count: _____
Date Started: _____
Date Finished: _____

📖 *WHY I CHOSE THIS BOOK:*
_____
_____

👑 *FAVORITE PART:*
(draw or describe)

🖋 *NOTES/REVIEW:*
_____
_____
_____
_____
_____
_____
_____
_____
_____
_____
_____
_____
_____
_____
_____
_____
_____

FICTION	NON-FICTION
Ease of Reading: ☆☆☆☆☆	*Ease of Reading:* ☆☆☆☆☆
Characters: ☆☆☆☆☆	*Substantiality:* ☆☆☆☆☆
Plot: ☆☆☆☆☆	*Impactfulness:* ☆☆☆☆☆

Overall Rating: ☆☆☆☆☆

🏅 *RECOMMEND?* ○ *Yes* ○ *No*

💡 *QUOTES/REFLECTIONS/EPIPHANIES:*
_____
_____
_____
_____
_____
_____
_____
_____

TITLE:

Author: _____ Publisher: _____

FORMAT: ○ Hardcover   ○ Paperback   ○ Ebook   ○ Audiobook
CATEGORY: ○ Fiction ○ Non-fiction Genre/Subject: _____
SOURCE: ○ Bought ○ Borrowed ○ Received from: _____

Page Count: _____
Date Started: _____
Date Finished: _____

WHY I CHOSE THIS BOOK:
_____
_____

♔ FAVORITE PART:
(draw or describe)

✎ NOTES/REVIEW:
_____
_____
_____
_____
_____
_____
_____
_____
_____
_____
_____
_____
_____
_____
_____
_____

FICTION	NON-FICTION
Ease of Reading:	Ease of Reading:
☆☆☆☆☆	☆☆☆☆☆
Characters:	Substantiality:
☆☆☆☆☆	☆☆☆☆☆
Plot:	Impactfulness:
☆☆☆☆☆	☆☆☆☆☆

Overall Rating: ☆☆☆☆☆

🎗 RECOMMEND? ○ Yes ○ No

💡 QUOTES/REFLECTIONS/EPIPHANIES:
_____
_____
_____
_____
_____
_____
_____
_____

📖 **TITLE:**

Author: _____ *Publisher:* _____

FORMAT: ○ *Hardcover*   ○ *Paperback*   ○ *Ebook*   ○ *Audiobook*
CATEGORY: ○ *Fiction* ○ *Non-fiction*   *Genre/Subject:* _____
SOURCE: ○ *Bought* ○ *Borrowed* ○ *Received from:* _____

Page Count: _____
Date Started: _____
Date Finished: _____

📖 *WHY I CHOSE THIS BOOK:*
_____
_____

♛ *FAVORITE PART:*
(draw or describe)

✒ *NOTES/REVIEW:*
_____
_____
_____
_____
_____
_____
_____
_____
_____
_____
_____
_____
_____
_____
_____
_____
_____

FICTION	NON-FICTION
Ease of Reading:	Ease of Reading:
☆☆☆☆☆	☆☆☆☆☆
Characters:	Substantiality:
☆☆☆☆☆	☆☆☆☆☆
Plot:	Impactfulness:
☆☆☆☆☆	☆☆☆☆☆

Overall Rating: ☆☆☆☆☆

🏅 *RECOMMEND?* ○ *Yes* ○ *No*

💡 *QUOTES/REFLECTIONS/EPIPHANIES:*
_____
_____
_____
_____
_____
_____
_____
_____

TITLE:

Author: _____ Publisher: _____

FORMAT: ○ Hardcover   ○ Paperback   ○ Ebook   ○ Audiobook
CATEGORY: ○ Fiction ○ Non-fiction Genre/Subject: _____
SOURCE: ○ Bought ○ Borrowed ○ Received from: _____

Page Count: _____
Date Started: _____
Date Finished: _____

WHY I CHOSE THIS BOOK:
_____
_____

♛ FAVORITE PART:
(draw or describe)

✎ NOTES/REVIEW:
_____
_____
_____
_____
_____
_____
_____
_____
_____
_____
_____
_____
_____
_____
_____
_____

FICTION	NON-FICTION
Ease of Reading: ☆☆☆☆☆	Ease of Reading: ☆☆☆☆☆
Characters: ☆☆☆☆☆	Substantiality: ☆☆☆☆☆
Plot: ☆☆☆☆☆	Impactfulness: ☆☆☆☆☆

Overall Rating: ☆☆☆☆☆

🏅 RECOMMEND?   ○ Yes   ○ No

💡 QUOTES/REFLECTIONS/EPIPHANIES:
_____
_____
_____
_____
_____
_____
_____
_____

TITLE:

Author: _____ *Publisher:* _____

FORMAT: ○ *Hardcover* ○ *Paperback* ○ *Ebook* ○ *Audiobook*
CATEGORY: ○ *Fiction* ○ *Non-fiction* *Genre/Subject:* _____
SOURCE: ○ *Bought* ○ *Borrowed* ○ *Received from:* _____

Page Count: _____
Date Started: _____
Date Finished: _____

📖 *WHY I CHOSE THIS BOOK:*
_____
_____

👑 *FAVORITE PART:*
(draw or describe)

✒ *NOTES/REVIEW:*
_____
_____
_____
_____
_____
_____
_____
_____
_____
_____
_____
_____
_____
_____
_____
_____
_____

FICTION	NON-FICTION
Ease of Reading:	*Ease of Reading:*
☆☆☆☆☆	☆☆☆☆☆
Characters:	*Substantiality:*
☆☆☆☆☆	☆☆☆☆☆
Plot:	*Impactfulness:*
☆☆☆☆☆	☆☆☆☆☆

Overall Rating: ☆☆☆☆☆

🏅 *RECOMMEND?* ○ *Yes* ○ *No*

💡 *QUOTES/REFLECTIONS/EPIPHANIES:*
_____
_____
_____
_____
_____
_____
_____
_____

TITLE:

Author: _____ *Publisher:* _____

FORMAT: ○ *Hardcover* ○ *Paperback* ○ *Ebook* ○ *Audiobook*
CATEGORY: ○ *Fiction* ○ *Non-fiction* *Genre/Subject:* _____
SOURCE: ○ *Bought* ○ *Borrowed* ○ *Received from:* _____

Page Count: _____
Date Started: _____
Date Finished: _____

📖 *WHY I CHOSE THIS BOOK:*
_____
_____

♛ *FAVORITE PART:*
(draw or describe)

✒ *NOTES/REVIEW:*
_____
_____
_____
_____
_____
_____
_____
_____
_____
_____
_____
_____
_____
_____
_____
_____
_____

FICTION	NON-FICTION
Ease of Reading:	Ease of Reading:
☆☆☆☆☆	☆☆☆☆☆
Characters:	Substantiality:
☆☆☆☆☆	☆☆☆☆☆
Plot:	Impactfulness:
☆☆☆☆☆	☆☆☆☆☆

Overall Rating: ☆☆☆☆☆

🏅 *RECOMMEND?* ○ *Yes* ○ *No*

💡 *QUOTES/REFLECTIONS/EPIPHANIES:*
_____
_____
_____
_____
_____
_____
_____
_____

 **TITLE:**

Author: _____ *Publisher:* _____

FORMAT: ○ *Hardcover*   ○ *Paperback*   ○ *Ebook*   ○ *Audiobook*
CATEGORY: ○ *Fiction* ○ *Non-fiction*   *Genre/Subject:* _____
SOURCE: ○ *Bought* ○ *Borrowed* ○ *Received from:* _____

Page Count: _____
Date Started: _____
Date Finished: _____

📖 *WHY I CHOSE THIS BOOK:*
_____
_____

👑 *FAVORITE PART:*
(draw or describe)

🖋 *NOTES/REVIEW:*
_____
_____
_____
_____
_____
_____
_____
_____
_____
_____
_____
_____
_____
_____
_____
_____

FICTION	NON-FICTION
Ease of Reading: ☆☆☆☆☆	*Ease of Reading:* ☆☆☆☆☆
Characters: ☆☆☆☆☆	*Substantiality:* ☆☆☆☆☆
Plot: ☆☆☆☆☆	*Impactfulness:* ☆☆☆☆☆

Overall Rating: ☆☆☆☆☆

🏅 *RECOMMEND?* ○ *Yes* ○ *No*

💡 *QUOTES/REFLECTIONS/EPIPHANIES:*
_____
_____
_____
_____
_____
_____
_____
_____

TITLE:

Author: _____   Publisher: _____

FORMAT: ○ Hardcover   ○ Paperback   ○ Ebook   ○ Audiobook
CATEGORY: ○ Fiction   ○ Non-fiction   Genre/Subject: _____
SOURCE: ○ Bought   ○ Borrowed   ○ Received from: _____

Page Count: _____
Date Started: _____
Date Finished: _____

WHY I CHOSE THIS BOOK:
_____
_____

FAVORITE PART:
(draw or describe)

NOTES/REVIEW:
_____
_____
_____
_____
_____
_____
_____
_____
_____
_____
_____
_____
_____
_____
_____
_____
_____

FICTION	NON-FICTION
Ease of Reading: ☆☆☆☆☆	Ease of Reading: ☆☆☆☆☆
Characters: ☆☆☆☆☆	Substantiality: ☆☆☆☆☆
Plot: ☆☆☆☆☆	Impactfulness: ☆☆☆☆☆

Overall Rating: ☆☆☆☆☆

RECOMMEND?   ○ Yes   ○ No

QUOTES/REFLECTIONS/EPIPHANIES:
_____
_____
_____
_____
_____
_____
_____
_____

TITLE:

Author: _____ *Publisher:* _____

FORMAT: ○ *Hardcover* ○ *Paperback* ○ *Ebook* ○ *Audiobook*
CATEGORY: ○ *Fiction* ○ *Non-fiction* *Genre/Subject:* _____
SOURCE: ○ *Bought* ○ *Borrowed* ○ *Received from:* _____

Page Count: _____
Date Started: _____
Date Finished: _____

WHY I CHOSE THIS BOOK:
_____
_____

FAVORITE PART:
(draw or describe)

NOTES/REVIEW:
_____
_____
_____
_____
_____
_____
_____
_____
_____
_____
_____
_____
_____
_____
_____
_____
_____

FICTION	NON-FICTION
Ease of Reading: ☆☆☆☆☆	*Ease of Reading:* ☆☆☆☆☆
Characters: ☆☆☆☆☆	*Substantiality:* ☆☆☆☆☆
Plot: ☆☆☆☆☆	*Impactfulness:* ☆☆☆☆☆

Overall Rating: ☆☆☆☆☆

RECOMMEND? ○ *Yes* ○ *No*

QUOTES/REFLECTIONS/EPIPHANIES:
_____
_____
_____
_____
_____
_____
_____
_____

📚 TITLE:

Author: _____ Publisher: _____

FORMAT: ○ Hardcover   ○ Paperback   ○ Ebook   ○ Audiobook
CATEGORY: ○ Fiction ○ Non-fiction   Genre/Subject: _____
SOURCE: ○ Bought ○ Borrowed ○ Received from: _____

Page Count: _____
Date Started: _____
Date Finished: _____

📖 WHY I CHOSE THIS BOOK:
_____
_____

👑 FAVORITE PART:
(draw or describe)

✒ NOTES/REVIEW:
_____
_____
_____
_____
_____
_____
_____
_____
_____
_____
_____
_____
_____
_____
_____
_____

FICTION	NON-FICTION
Ease of Reading: ☆☆☆☆☆	Ease of Reading: ☆☆☆☆☆
Characters: ☆☆☆☆☆	Substantiality: ☆☆☆☆☆
Plot: ☆☆☆☆☆	Impactfulness: ☆☆☆☆☆

Overall Rating: ☆☆☆☆☆

🏅 RECOMMEND? ○ Yes ○ No

💡 QUOTES/REFLECTIONS/EPIPHANIES:
_____
_____
_____
_____
_____
_____
_____
_____

TITLE:

Author: _____ *Publisher:* _____

FORMAT: ○ *Hardcover* ○ *Paperback* ○ *Ebook* ○ *Audiobook*
CATEGORY: ○ *Fiction* ○ *Non-fiction* *Genre/Subject:* _____
SOURCE: ○ *Bought* ○ *Borrowed* ○ *Received from:* _____

Page Count: _____
Date Started: _____
Date Finished: _____

📖 *WHY I CHOSE THIS BOOK:*
_____
_____

👑 *FAVORITE PART:*
(draw or describe)

✒ *NOTES/REVIEW:*
_____
_____
_____
_____
_____
_____
_____
_____
_____
_____
_____
_____
_____
_____
_____

FICTION	NON-FICTION
Ease of Reading:	Ease of Reading:
☆☆☆☆☆	☆☆☆☆☆
Characters:	Substantiality:
☆☆☆☆☆	☆☆☆☆☆
Plot:	Impactfulness:
☆☆☆☆☆	☆☆☆☆☆

Overall Rating: ☆☆☆☆☆

🎖 *RECOMMEND?* ○ *Yes* ○ *No*

💡 *QUOTES/REFLECTIONS/EPIPHANIES:*
_____
_____
_____
_____
_____
_____
_____

TITLE:

Author: _____ *Publisher:* _____

FORMAT: ○ *Hardcover* ○ *Paperback* ○ *Ebook* ○ *Audiobook*
CATEGORY: ○ *Fiction* ○ *Non-fiction* *Genre/Subject:* _____
SOURCE: ○ *Bought* ○ *Borrowed* ○ *Received from:* _____

Page Count: _____
Date Started: _____
Date Finished: _____

📖 *WHY I CHOSE THIS BOOK:*
_____
_____

♛ *FAVORITE PART:*
(draw or describe)

✎ *NOTES/REVIEW:*

FICTION	NON-FICTION
Ease of Reading: ☆☆☆☆☆	*Ease of Reading:* ☆☆☆☆☆
Characters: ☆☆☆☆☆	*Substantiality:* ☆☆☆☆☆
Plot: ☆☆☆☆☆	*Impactfulness:* ☆☆☆☆☆

Overall Rating: ☆☆☆☆☆

🏅 *RECOMMEND?* ○ *Yes* ○ *No*

💡 *QUOTES/REFLECTIONS/EPIPHANIES:*
_____
_____
_____
_____
_____
_____
_____
_____

TITLE:

Author: _____ *Publisher:* _____

FORMAT: ○ *Hardcover* ○ *Paperback* ○ *Ebook* ○ *Audiobook*
CATEGORY: ○ *Fiction* ○ *Non-fiction* *Genre/Subject:* _____
SOURCE: ○ *Bought* ○ *Borrowed* ○ *Received from:* _____

Page Count: _____
Date Started: _____
Date Finished: _____

📖 *WHY I CHOSE THIS BOOK:*
_____
_____

👑 *FAVORITE PART:*
(draw or describe)

🖋 *NOTES/REVIEW:*
_____
_____
_____
_____
_____
_____
_____
_____
_____
_____
_____
_____
_____
_____
_____
_____

FICTION	NON-FICTION
Ease of Reading:	Ease of Reading:
☆☆☆☆☆	☆☆☆☆☆
Characters:	Substantiality:
☆☆☆☆☆	☆☆☆☆☆
Plot:	Impactfulness:
☆☆☆☆☆	☆☆☆☆☆

Overall Rating: ☆☆☆☆☆

🏅 *RECOMMEND?* ○ *Yes* ○ *No*

💡 *QUOTES/REFLECTIONS/EPIPHANIES:*
_____
_____
_____
_____
_____
_____
_____
_____

TITLE:

Author: _____ Publisher: _____

FORMAT: ○ Hardcover ○ Paperback ○ Ebook ○ Audiobook
CATEGORY: ○ Fiction ○ Non-fiction Genre/Subject: _____
SOURCE: ○ Bought ○ Borrowed ○ Received from: _____

Page Count: _____
Date Started: _____
Date Finished: _____

WHY I CHOSE THIS BOOK:
_____
_____

♛ FAVORITE PART:
(draw or describe)

✎ NOTES/REVIEW:
_____
_____
_____
_____
_____
_____
_____
_____
_____
_____
_____
_____
_____
_____
_____

FICTION	NON-FICTION
Ease of Reading:	Ease of Reading:
☆☆☆☆☆	☆☆☆☆☆
Characters:	Substantiality:
☆☆☆☆☆	☆☆☆☆☆
Plot:	Impactfulness:
☆☆☆☆☆	☆☆☆☆☆

Overall Rating: ☆☆☆☆☆

🎗 RECOMMEND? ○ Yes ○ No

💡 QUOTES/REFLECTIONS/EPIPHANIES:
_____
_____
_____
_____
_____
_____
_____
_____

TITLE:

Author: _____ Publisher: _____

FORMAT: ○ Hardcover ○ Paperback ○ Ebook ○ Audiobook
CATEGORY: ○ Fiction ○ Non-fiction Genre/Subject: _____
SOURCE: ○ Bought ○ Borrowed ○ Received from: _____

Page Count: _____
Date Started: _____
Date Finished: _____

WHY I CHOSE THIS BOOK:
_____
_____

♛ FAVORITE PART:
(draw or describe)

✎ NOTES/REVIEW:
_____
_____
_____
_____
_____
_____
_____
_____
_____
_____
_____
_____
_____
_____
_____
_____

FICTION	NON-FICTION
Ease of Reading: ☆☆☆☆☆	Ease of Reading: ☆☆☆☆☆
Characters: ☆☆☆☆☆	Substantiality: ☆☆☆☆☆
Plot: ☆☆☆☆☆	Impactfulness: ☆☆☆☆☆

Overall Rating: ☆☆☆☆☆

🎖 RECOMMEND? ○ Yes ○ No

💡 QUOTES/REFLECTIONS/EPIPHANIES:
_____
_____
_____
_____
_____
_____
_____
_____

📚 TITLE:

Author: _____ Publisher: _____

FORMAT: ◯ Hardcover   ◯ Paperback   ◯ Ebook   ◯ Audiobook
CATEGORY: ◯ Fiction   ◯ Non-fiction   Genre/Subject: _____
SOURCE: ◯ Bought   ◯ Borrowed   ◯ Received from: _____

Page Count: _____
Date Started: _____
Date Finished: _____

📖 WHY I CHOSE THIS BOOK:
_____
_____

👑 FAVORITE PART:
(draw or describe)

🖋 NOTES/REVIEW:

FICTION	NON-FICTION
Ease of Reading: ☆☆☆☆☆	Ease of Reading: ☆☆☆☆☆
Characters: ☆☆☆☆☆	Substantiality: ☆☆☆☆☆
Plot: ☆☆☆☆☆	Impactfulness: ☆☆☆☆☆

Overall Rating: ☆☆☆☆☆

🏅 RECOMMEND?   ◯ Yes   ◯ No

💡 QUOTES/REFLECTIONS/EPIPHANIES:
_____
_____
_____
_____
_____
_____
_____
_____

📚 **TITLE:**

Author: _____ *Publisher:* _____

FORMAT: ○ *Hardcover* ○ *Paperback* ○ *Ebook* ○ *Audiobook*
CATEGORY: ○ *Fiction* ○ *Non-fiction* *Genre/Subject:* _____
SOURCE: ○ *Bought* ○ *Borrowed* ○ *Received from:* _____

Page Count: _____
Date Started: _____
Date Finished: _____

📖 *WHY I CHOSE THIS BOOK:*
_____
_____

👑 *FAVORITE PART:*
(draw or describe)

✒ *NOTES/REVIEW:*
_____
_____
_____
_____
_____
_____
_____
_____
_____
_____
_____
_____
_____

FICTION	NON-FICTION
Ease of Reading:	Ease of Reading:
☆☆☆☆☆	☆☆☆☆☆
Characters:	Substantiality:
☆☆☆☆☆	☆☆☆☆☆
Plot:	Impactfulness:
☆☆☆☆☆	☆☆☆☆☆

Overall Rating: ☆☆☆☆☆

🏅 *RECOMMEND?* ○ *Yes* ○ *No*

💡 *QUOTES/REFLECTIONS/EPIPHANIES:*
_____
_____
_____
_____
_____
_____
_____
_____

📚 **TITLE:**

Author: _____ *Publisher:* _____

FORMAT: ○ *Hardcover* ○ *Paperback* ○ *Ebook* ○ *Audiobook*
CATEGORY: ○ *Fiction* ○ *Non-fiction* *Genre/Subject:* _____
SOURCE: ○ *Bought* ○ *Borrowed* ○ *Received from:* _____

Page Count: _____
Date Started: _____
Date Finished: _____

📖 *WHY I CHOSE THIS BOOK:*
_____
_____

👑 *FAVORITE PART:*
(draw or describe)

🖋 *NOTES/REVIEW:*

FICTION	NON-FICTION
Ease of Reading:	Ease of Reading:
☆☆☆☆☆	☆☆☆☆☆
Characters:	Substantiality:
☆☆☆☆☆	☆☆☆☆☆
Plot:	Impactfulness:
☆☆☆☆☆	☆☆☆☆☆

Overall Rating: ☆☆☆☆☆

🎗 *RECOMMEND?* ○ *Yes* ○ *No*

💡 *QUOTES/REFLECTIONS/EPIPHANIES:*
_____
_____
_____
_____
_____
_____
_____

TITLE:

Author: _____ Publisher: _____

FORMAT: ○ Hardcover ○ Paperback ○ Ebook ○ Audiobook
CATEGORY: ○ Fiction ○ Non-fiction Genre/Subject: _____
SOURCE: ○ Bought ○ Borrowed ○ Received from: _____

Page Count: _____
Date Started: _____
Date Finished: _____

WHY I CHOSE THIS BOOK:
_____
_____

♔ FAVORITE PART:
(draw or describe)

✒ NOTES/REVIEW:
_____
_____
_____
_____
_____
_____
_____
_____
_____
_____
_____
_____
_____
_____
_____
_____

FICTION	NON-FICTION
Ease of Reading:	Ease of Reading:
☆☆☆☆☆	☆☆☆☆☆
Characters:	Substantiality:
☆☆☆☆☆	☆☆☆☆☆
Plot:	Impactfulness:
☆☆☆☆☆	☆☆☆☆☆

Overall Rating: ☆☆☆☆☆

🎖 RECOMMEND? ○ Yes ○ No

💡 QUOTES/REFLECTIONS/EPIPHANIES:
_____
_____
_____
_____
_____
_____
_____
_____

TITLE:

Author: _____ Publisher: _____

FORMAT: ○ Hardcover ○ Paperback ○ Ebook ○ Audiobook
CATEGORY: ○ Fiction ○ Non-fiction Genre/Subject: _____
SOURCE: ○ Bought ○ Borrowed ○ Received from: _____

Page Count: _____
Date Started: _____
Date Finished: _____

📖 WHY I CHOSE THIS BOOK:
_____
_____

👑 FAVORITE PART:
(draw or describe)

✍ NOTES/REVIEW:
_____
_____
_____
_____
_____
_____
_____
_____
_____
_____
_____
_____
_____
_____
_____
_____
_____
_____

FICTION	NON-FICTION
Ease of Reading: ☆☆☆☆☆	Ease of Reading: ☆☆☆☆☆
Characters: ☆☆☆☆☆	Substantiality: ☆☆☆☆☆
Plot: ☆☆☆☆☆	Impactfulness: ☆☆☆☆☆

Overall Rating: ☆☆☆☆☆

🎗 RECOMMEND? ○ Yes ○ No

💡 QUOTES/REFLECTIONS/EPIPHANIES:
_____
_____
_____
_____
_____
_____
_____
_____

📚 **TITLE:**

Author: _____ *Publisher:* _____

FORMAT: ○ *Hardcover*   ○ *Paperback*   ○ *Ebook*   ○ *Audiobook*
CATEGORY: ○ *Fiction* ○ *Non-fiction*   *Genre/Subject:* _____
SOURCE: ○ *Bought* ○ *Borrowed* ○ *Received from:* _____

Page Count: _____
Date Started: _____
Date Finished: _____

📖 *WHY I CHOSE THIS BOOK:*
_____
_____

👑 *FAVORITE PART:*
(draw or describe)

✒ *NOTES/REVIEW:*
_____
_____
_____
_____
_____
_____
_____
_____
_____
_____
_____
_____
_____
_____
_____
_____
_____

FICTION	NON-FICTION
Ease of Reading: ☆☆☆☆☆	*Ease of Reading:* ☆☆☆☆☆
Characters: ☆☆☆☆☆	*Substantiality:* ☆☆☆☆☆
Plot: ☆☆☆☆☆	*Impactfulness:* ☆☆☆☆☆

Overall Rating: ☆☆☆☆☆

🏅 *RECOMMEND?* ○ *Yes* ○ *No*

💡 *QUOTES/REFLECTIONS/EPIPHANIES:*
_____
_____
_____
_____
_____
_____
_____
_____

📚 **TITLE:**

Author: _____ *Publisher:* _____

FORMAT: ○ *Hardcover*   ○ *Paperback*   ○ *Ebook*   ○ *Audiobook*
CATEGORY: ○ *Fiction* ○ *Non-fiction*   *Genre/Subject:* _____
SOURCE: ○ *Bought* ○ *Borrowed* ○ *Received from:* _____

Page Count: _____
Date Started: _____
Date Finished: _____

📖 *WHY I CHOSE THIS BOOK:*
_____
_____

👑 *FAVORITE PART:*
(draw or describe)

✒ *NOTES/REVIEW:*
_____
_____
_____
_____
_____
_____
_____
_____
_____
_____
_____
_____
_____
_____
_____

FICTION	NON-FICTION
Ease of Reading: ☆☆☆☆☆	*Ease of Reading:* ☆☆☆☆☆
Characters: ☆☆☆☆☆	*Substantiality:* ☆☆☆☆☆
Plot: ☆☆☆☆☆	*Impactfulness:* ☆☆☆☆☆

Overall Rating: ☆☆☆☆☆

🏅 *RECOMMEND?*   ○ *Yes*   ○ *No*

💡 *QUOTES/REFLECTIONS/EPIPHANIES:*
_____
_____
_____
_____
_____
_____
_____
_____

📚 **TITLE:**

Author: _____ *Publisher:* _____

FORMAT: ○ *Hardcover* ○ *Paperback* ○ *Ebook* ○ *Audiobook*
CATEGORY: ○ *Fiction* ○ *Non-fiction* *Genre/Subject:* _____
SOURCE: ○ *Bought* ○ *Borrowed* ○ *Received from:* _____

Page Count: _____
Date Started: _____
Date Finished: _____

📖 *WHY I CHOSE THIS BOOK:*
_____
_____

👑 *FAVORITE PART:*
(draw or describe)

✒ *NOTES/REVIEW:*
_____
_____
_____
_____
_____
_____
_____
_____
_____
_____
_____
_____
_____
_____
_____

FICTION	NON-FICTION
Ease of Reading:	*Ease of Reading:*
☆☆☆☆☆	☆☆☆☆☆
Characters:	*Substantiality:*
☆☆☆☆☆	☆☆☆☆☆
Plot:	*Impactfulness:*
☆☆☆☆☆	☆☆☆☆☆

Overall Rating: ☆☆☆☆☆

🏅 *RECOMMEND?* ○ *Yes* ○ *No*

💡 *QUOTES/REFLECTIONS/EPIPHANIES:*
_____
_____
_____
_____
_____
_____
_____
_____

TITLE:

Author: _____ Publisher: _____

FORMAT: ○ Hardcover ○ Paperback ○ Ebook ○ Audiobook
CATEGORY: ○ Fiction ○ Non-fiction Genre/Subject: _____
SOURCE: ○ Bought ○ Borrowed ○ Received from: _____

Page Count: _____
Date Started: _____
Date Finished: _____

📖 WHY I CHOSE THIS BOOK:
_____
_____

👑 FAVORITE PART:
(draw or describe)

✍ NOTES/REVIEW:
_____
_____
_____
_____
_____
_____
_____
_____
_____
_____
_____
_____
_____
_____
_____
_____
_____

FICTION	NON-FICTION
Ease of Reading:	Ease of Reading:
☆☆☆☆☆	☆☆☆☆☆
Characters:	Substantiality:
☆☆☆☆☆	☆☆☆☆☆
Plot:	Impactfulness:
☆☆☆☆☆	☆☆☆☆☆

Overall Rating: ☆☆☆☆☆

🎗 RECOMMEND? ○ Yes ○ No

💡 QUOTES/REFLECTIONS/EPIPHANIES:
_____
_____
_____
_____
_____
_____
_____
_____

📚 **TITLE:**

Author: _____ *Publisher:* _____

FORMAT: ○ *Hardcover* ○ *Paperback* ○ *Ebook* ○ *Audiobook*
CATEGORY: ○ *Fiction* ○ *Non-fiction* *Genre/Subject:* _____
SOURCE: ○ *Bought* ○ *Borrowed* ○ *Received from:* _____

Page Count: _____
Date Started: _____
Date Finished: _____

📖 *WHY I CHOSE THIS BOOK:*
_____
_____

👑 *FAVORITE PART:*
(draw or describe)

🖋 *NOTES/REVIEW:*
_____
_____
_____
_____
_____
_____
_____
_____
_____
_____
_____
_____
_____
_____
_____
_____

FICTION	*NON-FICTION*
Ease of Reading: ☆☆☆☆☆	Ease of Reading: ☆☆☆☆☆
Characters: ☆☆☆☆☆	Substantiality: ☆☆☆☆☆
Plot: ☆☆☆☆☆	Impactfulness: ☆☆☆☆☆

Overall Rating: ☆☆☆☆☆

🎖 *RECOMMEND?* ○ *Yes* ○ *No*

💡 *QUOTES/REFLECTIONS/EPIPHANIES:*
_____
_____
_____
_____
_____
_____
_____
_____

📚 TITLE:

Author: _____ *Publisher:* _____

FORMAT: ○ *Hardcover*   ○ *Paperback*   ○ *Ebook*   ○ *Audiobook*
CATEGORY: ○ *Fiction* ○ *Non-fiction* *Genre/Subject:* _____
SOURCE: ○ *Bought* ○ *Borrowed* ○ *Received from:* _____

Page Count: _____
Date Started: _____
Date Finished: _____

📖 *WHY I CHOSE THIS BOOK:*
_____
_____

👑 *FAVORITE PART:*
(draw or describe)

✒ *NOTES/REVIEW:*
_____
_____
_____
_____
_____
_____
_____
_____
_____
_____
_____
_____
_____
_____
_____
_____
_____

FICTION	NON-FICTION
Ease of Reading:	Ease of Reading:
☆☆☆☆☆	☆☆☆☆☆
Characters:	Substantiality:
☆☆☆☆☆	☆☆☆☆☆
Plot:	Impactfulness:
☆☆☆☆☆	☆☆☆☆☆

Overall Rating: ☆☆☆☆☆

🏅 *RECOMMEND?*   ○ *Yes*   ○ *No*

💡 *QUOTES/REFLECTIONS/EPIPHANIES:*
_____
_____
_____
_____
_____
_____
_____
_____

TITLE:

Author: _____ Publisher: _____

FORMAT: ○ Hardcover   ○ Paperback   ○ Ebook   ○ Audiobook
CATEGORY: ○ Fiction ○ Non-fiction Genre/Subject: _____
SOURCE: ○ Bought ○ Borrowed ○ Received from: _____

Page Count: _____
Date Started: _____
Date Finished: _____

WHY I CHOSE THIS BOOK:
_____
_____

♛ FAVORITE PART:
(draw or describe)

✒ NOTES/REVIEW:
_____
_____
_____
_____
_____
_____
_____
_____
_____
_____
_____
_____
_____
_____

FICTION	NON-FICTION
Ease of Reading:	Ease of Reading:
☆☆☆☆☆	☆☆☆☆☆
Characters:	Substantiality:
☆☆☆☆☆	☆☆☆☆☆
Plot:	Impactfulness:
☆☆☆☆☆	☆☆☆☆☆

Overall Rating: ☆☆☆☆☆

🏅 RECOMMEND?   ○ Yes   ○ No

💡 QUOTES/REFLECTIONS/EPIPHANIES:
_____
_____
_____
_____
_____
_____
_____
_____

TITLE:

Author: _____ Publisher: _____

FORMAT: ○ Hardcover ○ Paperback ○ Ebook ○ Audiobook
CATEGORY: ○ Fiction ○ Non-fiction Genre/Subject: _____
SOURCE: ○ Bought ○ Borrowed ○ Received from: _____

Page Count: _____
Date Started: _____
Date Finished: _____

WHY I CHOSE THIS BOOK:
_____
_____

♔ **FAVORITE PART:**
(draw or describe)

✎ **NOTES/REVIEW:**
_____
_____
_____
_____
_____
_____
_____
_____
_____
_____
_____
_____
_____
_____
_____
_____
_____
_____
_____

FICTION	NON-FICTION
Ease of Reading:	Ease of Reading:
☆☆☆☆☆	☆☆☆☆☆
Characters:	Substantiality:
☆☆☆☆☆	☆☆☆☆☆
Plot:	Impactfulness:
☆☆☆☆☆	☆☆☆☆☆

Overall Rating: ☆☆☆☆☆

🎗 **RECOMMEND?** ○ Yes ○ No

💡 **QUOTES/REFLECTIONS/EPIPHANIES:**
_____
_____
_____
_____
_____
_____
_____
_____

📚 **TITLE:**

Author: _____ *Publisher:* _____

FORMAT: ○ *Hardcover* ○ *Paperback* ○ *Ebook* ○ *Audiobook*
CATEGORY: ○ *Fiction* ○ *Non-fiction* *Genre/Subject:* _____
SOURCE: ○ *Bought* ○ *Borrowed* ○ *Received from:* _____

Page Count: _____
Date Started: _____
Date Finished: _____

📖 *WHY I CHOSE THIS BOOK:*
_____
_____

👑 *FAVORITE PART:*
(draw or describe)

✒ *NOTES/REVIEW:*
_____
_____
_____
_____
_____
_____
_____
_____
_____
_____
_____
_____
_____
_____
_____

FICTION	NON-FICTION
Ease of Reading:	Ease of Reading:
☆☆☆☆☆	☆☆☆☆☆
Characters:	Substantiality:
☆☆☆☆☆	☆☆☆☆☆
Plot:	Impactfulness:
☆☆☆☆☆	☆☆☆☆☆

Overall Rating: ☆☆☆☆☆

🎗 *RECOMMEND?* ○ *Yes* ○ *No*

💡 *QUOTES/REFLECTIONS/EPIPHANIES:*
_____
_____
_____
_____
_____
_____
_____
_____

TITLE:

Author: _____ Publisher: _____

FORMAT: ○ Hardcover ○ Paperback ○ Ebook ○ Audiobook
CATEGORY: ○ Fiction ○ Non-fiction Genre/Subject: _____
SOURCE: ○ Bought ○ Borrowed ○ Received from: _____

Page Count: _____
Date Started: _____
Date Finished: _____

WHY I CHOSE THIS BOOK:
_____
_____

♛ FAVORITE PART:
(draw or describe)

✍ NOTES/REVIEW:
_____
_____
_____
_____
_____
_____
_____
_____
_____
_____
_____
_____
_____
_____
_____
_____

FICTION	NON-FICTION
Ease of Reading:	Ease of Reading:
☆☆☆☆☆	☆☆☆☆☆
Characters:	Substantiality:
☆☆☆☆☆	☆☆☆☆☆
Plot:	Impactfulness:
☆☆☆☆☆	☆☆☆☆☆

Overall Rating: ☆☆☆☆☆

⚜ RECOMMEND? ○ Yes ○ No

💡 QUOTES/REFLECTIONS/EPIPHANIES:
_____
_____
_____
_____
_____
_____
_____
_____

TITLE:

Author: _____ Publisher: _____

FORMAT: ○ Hardcover ○ Paperback ○ Ebook ○ Audiobook
CATEGORY: ○ Fiction ○ Non-fiction Genre/Subject: _____
SOURCE: ○ Bought ○ Borrowed ○ Received from: _____

Page Count: _____
Date Started: _____
Date Finished: _____

WHY I CHOSE THIS BOOK:
_____
_____

♔ FAVORITE PART:
(draw or describe)

✎ NOTES/REVIEW:
_____
_____
_____
_____
_____
_____
_____
_____
_____
_____
_____
_____
_____
_____

FICTION	NON-FICTION
Ease of Reading: ☆☆☆☆☆	Ease of Reading: ☆☆☆☆☆
Characters: ☆☆☆☆☆	Substantiality: ☆☆☆☆☆
Plot: ☆☆☆☆☆	Impactfulness: ☆☆☆☆☆

Overall Rating: ☆☆☆☆☆

⚜ RECOMMEND? ○ Yes ○ No

💡 QUOTES/REFLECTIONS/EPIPHANIES:
_____
_____
_____
_____
_____
_____
_____
_____

📚 **TITLE:**

Author: _____ *Publisher:* _____

FORMAT: ○ *Hardcover* ○ *Paperback* ○ *Ebook* ○ *Audiobook*
CATEGORY: ○ *Fiction* ○ *Non-fiction* *Genre/Subject:* _____
SOURCE: ○ *Bought* ○ *Borrowed* ○ *Received from:* _____

Page Count: _____
Date Started: _____
Date Finished: _____

📖 *WHY I CHOSE THIS BOOK:*
_____
_____

👑 *FAVORITE PART:*
(draw or describe)

✒️ *NOTES/REVIEW:*
_____
_____
_____
_____
_____
_____
_____
_____
_____
_____
_____
_____
_____
_____
_____
_____
_____

FICTION	NON-FICTION
Ease of Reading: ☆☆☆☆☆	*Ease of Reading:* ☆☆☆☆☆
Characters: ☆☆☆☆☆	*Substantiality:* ☆☆☆☆☆
Plot: ☆☆☆☆☆	*Impactfulness:* ☆☆☆☆☆

Overall Rating: ☆☆☆☆☆

🎖️ *RECOMMEND?* ○ *Yes* ○ *No*

💡 *QUOTES/REFLECTIONS/EPIPHANIES:*
_____
_____
_____
_____
_____
_____
_____
_____

TITLE:

Author: _____ *Publisher:* _____

FORMAT: ○ *Hardcover* ○ *Paperback* ○ *Ebook* ○ *Audiobook*
CATEGORY: ○ *Fiction* ○ *Non-fiction* *Genre/Subject:* _____
SOURCE: ○ *Bought* ○ *Borrowed* ○ *Received from:* _____

Page Count: _____
Date Started: _____
Date Finished: _____

WHY I CHOSE THIS BOOK:

_____
_____

FAVORITE PART:
(draw or describe)

NOTES/REVIEW:

_____
_____
_____
_____
_____
_____
_____
_____
_____
_____
_____
_____
_____
_____
_____
_____
_____

FICTION	NON-FICTION
Ease of Reading: ☆☆☆☆☆	*Ease of Reading:* ☆☆☆☆☆
Characters: ☆☆☆☆☆	*Substantiality:* ☆☆☆☆☆
Plot: ☆☆☆☆☆	*Impactfulness:* ☆☆☆☆☆

Overall Rating: ☆☆☆☆☆

RECOMMEND? ○ *Yes* ○ *No*

QUOTES/REFLECTIONS/EPIPHANIES:

_____
_____
_____
_____
_____
_____
_____
_____

TITLE:

Author: _____ *Publisher:* _____

FORMAT: ○ *Hardcover* ○ *Paperback* ○ *Ebook* ○ *Audiobook*
CATEGORY: ○ *Fiction* ○ *Non-fiction* *Genre/Subject:* _____
SOURCE: ○ *Bought* ○ *Borrowed* ○ *Received from:* _____

Page Count: _____
Date Started: _____
Date Finished: _____

WHY I CHOSE THIS BOOK:
_____
_____

♛ *FAVORITE PART:*
(draw or describe)

✍ *NOTES/REVIEW:*
_____
_____
_____
_____
_____
_____
_____
_____
_____
_____
_____
_____
_____
_____
_____
_____

FICTION	NON-FICTION
Ease of Reading:	*Ease of Reading:*
☆☆☆☆☆	☆☆☆☆☆
Characters:	*Substantiality:*
☆☆☆☆☆	☆☆☆☆☆
Plot:	*Impactfulness:*
☆☆☆☆☆	☆☆☆☆☆

Overall Rating: ☆☆☆☆☆

🎗 *RECOMMEND?* ○ *Yes* ○ *No*

💡 *QUOTES/REFLECTIONS/EPIPHANIES:*
_____
_____
_____
_____
_____
_____
_____
_____

TITLE:

Author: _____ Publisher: _____

FORMAT: ○ Hardcover ○ Paperback ○ Ebook ○ Audiobook
CATEGORY: ○ Fiction ○ Non-fiction Genre/Subject: _____
SOURCE: ○ Bought ○ Borrowed ○ Received from: _____

Page Count: _____
Date Started: _____
Date Finished: _____

📖 WHY I CHOSE THIS BOOK:
_____
_____

👑 FAVORITE PART:
(draw or describe)

✒ NOTES/REVIEW:
_____
_____
_____
_____
_____
_____
_____
_____
_____
_____
_____
_____
_____
_____
_____
_____
_____

FICTION	NON-FICTION
Ease of Reading:	Ease of Reading:
☆☆☆☆☆	☆☆☆☆☆
Characters:	Substantiality:
☆☆☆☆☆	☆☆☆☆☆
Plot:	Impactfulness:
☆☆☆☆☆	☆☆☆☆☆

Overall Rating: ☆☆☆☆☆

🎖 RECOMMEND? ○ Yes ○ No

💡 QUOTES/REFLECTIONS/EPIPHANIES:

_____
_____
_____
_____
_____
_____
_____
_____

TITLE:

Author: _____ Publisher: _____

FORMAT: ○ Hardcover ○ Paperback ○ Ebook ○ Audiobook
CATEGORY: ○ Fiction ○ Non-fiction Genre/Subject: _____
SOURCE: ○ Bought ○ Borrowed ○ Received from: _____

Page Count: _____
Date Started: _____
Date Finished: _____

📖 WHY I CHOSE THIS BOOK:
_____
_____

👑 FAVORITE PART:
(draw or describe)

✒️ NOTES/REVIEW:
_____
_____
_____
_____
_____
_____
_____
_____
_____
_____
_____
_____
_____
_____
_____
_____

FICTION	NON-FICTION
Ease of Reading:	Ease of Reading:
☆☆☆☆☆	☆☆☆☆☆
Characters:	Substantiality:
☆☆☆☆☆	☆☆☆☆☆
Plot:	Impactfulness:
☆☆☆☆☆	☆☆☆☆☆

Overall Rating: ☆☆☆☆☆

🏅 RECOMMEND? ○ Yes ○ No

💡 QUOTES/REFLECTIONS/EPIPHANIES:
_____
_____
_____
_____
_____
_____
_____
_____

TITLE:

Author: _____ Publisher: _____

FORMAT: ○ Hardcover   ○ Paperback   ○ Ebook   ○ Audiobook
CATEGORY: ○ Fiction ○ Non-fiction   Genre/Subject: _____
SOURCE: ○ Bought ○ Borrowed ○ Received from: _____

Page Count: _____
Date Started: _____
Date Finished: _____

📖 WHY I CHOSE THIS BOOK:
_____
_____

👑 FAVORITE PART:
(draw or describe)

✍ NOTES/REVIEW:
_____
_____
_____
_____
_____
_____
_____
_____
_____
_____
_____
_____
_____
_____
_____
_____
_____

FICTION	NON-FICTION
Ease of Reading:	Ease of Reading:
☆☆☆☆☆	☆☆☆☆☆
Characters:	Substantiality:
☆☆☆☆☆	☆☆☆☆☆
Plot:	Impactfulness:
☆☆☆☆☆	☆☆☆☆☆
Overall Rating: ☆☆☆☆☆	

🎗 RECOMMEND?   ○ Yes   ○ No

💡 QUOTES/REFLECTIONS/EPIPHANIES:
_____
_____
_____
_____
_____
_____
_____
_____

📚 TITLE:

Author: _____ *Publisher:* _____

FORMAT: ○ *Hardcover*   ○ *Paperback*   ○ *Ebook*   ○ *Audiobook*
CATEGORY: ○ *Fiction* ○ *Non-fiction*   *Genre/Subject:* _____
SOURCE: ○ *Bought* ○ *Borrowed* ○ *Received from:* _____

Page Count: _____
Date Started: _____
Date Finished: _____

📖 *WHY I CHOSE THIS BOOK:*
_____
_____

👑 *FAVORITE PART:*
(draw or describe)

✒ *NOTES/REVIEW:*
_____
_____
_____
_____
_____
_____
_____
_____
_____
_____
_____
_____
_____
_____
_____
_____
_____

FICTION	NON-FICTION
Ease of Reading:	Ease of Reading:
☆☆☆☆☆	☆☆☆☆☆
Characters:	Substantiality:
☆☆☆☆☆	☆☆☆☆☆
Plot:	Impactfulness:
☆☆☆☆☆	☆☆☆☆☆

Overall Rating: ☆☆☆☆☆

🎗 *RECOMMEND?*   ○ *Yes*   ○ *No*

💡 *QUOTES/REFLECTIONS/EPIPHANIES:*
_____
_____
_____
_____
_____
_____
_____
_____

 **TITLE:**

Author: _____ *Publisher:* _____

FORMAT: ○ *Hardcover*   ○ *Paperback*   ○ *Ebook*   ○ *Audiobook*
CATEGORY: ○ *Fiction* ○ *Non-fiction* Genre/Subject: _____
SOURCE: ○ *Bought* ○ *Borrowed* ○ *Received from:* _____

Page Count: _____
Date Started: _____
Date Finished: _____

📖 *WHY I CHOSE THIS BOOK:*
_____
_____

♛ *FAVORITE PART:*
(draw or describe)

✒ *NOTES/REVIEW:*
_____
_____
_____
_____
_____
_____
_____
_____
_____
_____
_____
_____
_____
_____
_____
_____
_____
_____

FICTION	NON-FICTION
Ease of Reading:	Ease of Reading:
☆☆☆☆☆	☆☆☆☆☆
Characters:	Substantiality:
☆☆☆☆☆	☆☆☆☆☆
Plot:	Impactfulness:
☆☆☆☆☆	☆☆☆☆☆

Overall Rating: ☆☆☆☆☆

🏅 *RECOMMEND?* ○ *Yes* ○ *No*

💡 *QUOTES/REFLECTIONS/EPIPHANIES:*
_____
_____
_____
_____
_____
_____
_____
_____
_____

📚 **TITLE:**

Author: _____ *Publisher:* _____

FORMAT: ○ *Hardcover* ○ *Paperback* ○ *Ebook* ○ *Audiobook*
CATEGORY: ○ *Fiction* ○ *Non-fiction* *Genre/Subject:* _____
SOURCE: ○ *Bought* ○ *Borrowed* ○ *Received from:* _____

Page Count: _____
Date Started: _____
Date Finished: _____

📖 *WHY I CHOSE THIS BOOK:*
_____
_____

♛ *FAVORITE PART:*
(draw or describe)

✒ *NOTES/REVIEW:*
_____
_____
_____
_____
_____
_____
_____
_____
_____
_____
_____
_____
_____
_____
_____
_____

FICTION	NON-FICTION
Ease of Reading: ☆☆☆☆☆	*Ease of Reading:* ☆☆☆☆☆
Characters: ☆☆☆☆☆	*Substantiality:* ☆☆☆☆☆
Plot: ☆☆☆☆☆	*Impactfulness:* ☆☆☆☆☆

Overall Rating: ☆☆☆☆☆

🎖 *RECOMMEND?* ○ *Yes* ○ *No*

💡 *QUOTES/REFLECTIONS/EPIPHANIES:*
_____
_____
_____
_____
_____
_____
_____
_____

TITLE:

Author: _____ Publisher: _____

FORMAT: ○ Hardcover　　○ Paperback　　○ Ebook　　○ Audiobook
CATEGORY: ○ Fiction ○ Non-fiction　Genre/Subject: _____
SOURCE: ○ Bought　○ Borrowed　○ Received from: _____

Page Count: _____
Date Started: _____
Date Finished: _____

📖 WHY I CHOSE THIS BOOK:
_____
_____

👑 FAVORITE PART:
(draw or describe)

✒ NOTES/REVIEW:
_____
_____
_____
_____
_____
_____
_____
_____
_____
_____
_____
_____
_____
_____
_____

FICTION	NON-FICTION
Ease of Reading:	Ease of Reading:
☆☆☆☆☆	☆☆☆☆☆
Characters:	Substantiality:
☆☆☆☆☆	☆☆☆☆☆
Plot:	Impactfulness:
☆☆☆☆☆	☆☆☆☆☆
Overall Rating: ☆☆☆☆☆	

🏅 RECOMMEND?　○ Yes　○ No

💡 QUOTES/REFLECTIONS/EPIPHANIES:
_____
_____
_____
_____
_____
_____
_____
_____

TITLE:

Author: _____ Publisher: _____

FORMAT: ○ Hardcover ○ Paperback ○ Ebook ○ Audiobook
CATEGORY: ○ Fiction ○ Non-fiction Genre/Subject: _____
SOURCE: ○ Bought ○ Borrowed ○ Received from: _____

Page Count: _____
Date Started: _____
Date Finished: _____

WHY I CHOSE THIS BOOK:
_____
_____

♛ FAVORITE PART:
(draw or describe)

✎ NOTES/REVIEW:
_____
_____
_____
_____
_____
_____
_____
_____
_____
_____
_____
_____
_____
_____
_____
_____

FICTION	NON-FICTION
Ease of Reading:	Ease of Reading:
☆☆☆☆☆	☆☆☆☆☆
Characters:	Substantiality:
☆☆☆☆☆	☆☆☆☆☆
Plot:	Impactfulness:
☆☆☆☆☆	☆☆☆☆☆

Overall Rating: ☆☆☆☆☆

⚜ RECOMMEND? ○ Yes ○ No

💡 QUOTES/REFLECTIONS/EPIPHANIES:
_____
_____
_____
_____
_____
_____
_____

📚 TITLE:

Author: _____ *Publisher:* _____

FORMAT: ○ *Hardcover*　　○ *Paperback*　　○ *Ebook*　　○ *Audiobook*
CATEGORY: ○ *Fiction* ○ *Non-fiction*　*Genre/Subject:* _____
SOURCE: ○ *Bought* ○ *Borrowed* ○ *Received from:* _____

Page Count: _____
Date Started: _____
Date Finished: _____

📖 *WHY I CHOSE THIS BOOK:*
_____
_____

👑 *FAVORITE PART:*
(draw or describe)

✒ *NOTES/REVIEW:*

FICTION	NON-FICTION
Ease of Reading: ☆☆☆☆☆	*Ease of Reading:* ☆☆☆☆☆
Characters: ☆☆☆☆☆	*Substantiality:* ☆☆☆☆☆
Plot: ☆☆☆☆☆	*Impactfulness:* ☆☆☆☆☆

Overall Rating: ☆☆☆☆☆

🏅 *RECOMMEND?* ○ *Yes* ○ *No*

💡 *QUOTES/REFLECTIONS/EPIPHANIES:*
_____
_____
_____
_____
_____
_____
_____
_____

TITLE:

Author: _____ Publisher: _____

FORMAT: ○ Hardcover   ○ Paperback   ○ Ebook   ○ Audiobook
CATEGORY: ○ Fiction ○ Non-fiction   Genre/Subject: _____
SOURCE: ○ Bought ○ Borrowed ○ Received from: _____

Page Count: _____
Date Started: _____
Date Finished: _____

WHY I CHOSE THIS BOOK:
_____
_____

♔ FAVORITE PART:
(draw or describe)

✒ NOTES/REVIEW:
_____
_____
_____
_____
_____
_____
_____
_____
_____
_____
_____
_____
_____
_____
_____

FICTION	NON-FICTION
Ease of Reading:	Ease of Reading:
☆☆☆☆☆	☆☆☆☆☆
Characters:	Substantiality:
☆☆☆☆☆	☆☆☆☆☆
Plot:	Impactfulness:
☆☆☆☆☆	☆☆☆☆☆

Overall Rating: ☆☆☆☆☆

🎖 RECOMMEND?   ○ Yes   ○ No

💡 QUOTES/REFLECTIONS/EPIPHANIES:
_____
_____
_____
_____
_____
_____
_____
_____

📚 **TITLE:**

Author: _____ *Publisher:* _____

FORMAT: ○ *Hardcover* ○ *Paperback* ○ *Ebook* ○ *Audiobook*
CATEGORY: ○ *Fiction* ○ *Non-fiction* *Genre/Subject:* _____
SOURCE: ○ *Bought* ○ *Borrowed* ○ *Received from:* _____

Page Count: _____
Date Started: _____
Date Finished: _____

📖 *WHY I CHOSE THIS BOOK:*
_____
_____

👑 *FAVORITE PART:*
(draw or describe)

✒️ *NOTES/REVIEW:*
_____
_____
_____
_____
_____
_____
_____
_____
_____
_____
_____
_____
_____
_____
_____

FICTION	NON-FICTION
Ease of Reading:	*Ease of Reading:*
☆☆☆☆☆	☆☆☆☆☆
Characters:	*Substantiality:*
☆☆☆☆☆	☆☆☆☆☆
Plot:	*Impactfulness:*
☆☆☆☆☆	☆☆☆☆☆

Overall Rating: ☆☆☆☆☆

🎗️ *RECOMMEND?* ○ *Yes* ○ *No*

💡 *QUOTES/REFLECTIONS/EPIPHANIES:*
_____
_____
_____
_____
_____
_____
_____
_____

📚 **TITLE:**

Author: _____ *Publisher:* _____

FORMAT: ○ *Hardcover* ○ *Paperback* ○ *Ebook* ○ *Audiobook*
CATEGORY: ○ *Fiction* ○ *Non-fiction* *Genre/Subject:* _____
SOURCE: ○ *Bought* ○ *Borrowed* ○ *Received from:* _____

Page Count: _____
Date Started: _____
Date Finished: _____

📖 *WHY I CHOSE THIS BOOK:*
_____
_____

♛ *FAVORITE PART:*
(draw or describe)

✒ *NOTES/REVIEW:*
_____
_____
_____
_____
_____
_____
_____
_____
_____
_____
_____
_____
_____
_____
_____
_____
_____

FICTION	NON-FICTION
Ease of Reading:	Ease of Reading:
☆☆☆☆☆	☆☆☆☆☆
Characters:	Substantiality:
☆☆☆☆☆	☆☆☆☆☆
Plot:	Impactfulness:
☆☆☆☆☆	☆☆☆☆☆

Overall Rating: ☆☆☆☆☆

🏅 *RECOMMEND?* ○ *Yes* ○ *No*

💡 *QUOTES/REFLECTIONS/EPIPHANIES:*
_____
_____
_____
_____
_____
_____
_____

TITLE:

Author: _____ *Publisher:* _____

FORMAT: ○ *Hardcover* ○ *Paperback* ○ *Ebook* ○ *Audiobook*
CATEGORY: ○ *Fiction* ○ *Non-fiction* *Genre/Subject:* _____
SOURCE: ○ *Bought* ○ *Borrowed* ○ *Received from:* _____

Page Count: _____
Date Started: _____
Date Finished: _____

WHY I CHOSE THIS BOOK:
_____
_____

FAVORITE PART:
(draw or describe)

NOTES/REVIEW:
_____
_____
_____
_____
_____
_____
_____
_____
_____
_____
_____
_____
_____
_____
_____
_____

FICTION	*NON-FICTION*
Ease of Reading: ☆☆☆☆☆	*Ease of Reading:* ☆☆☆☆☆
Characters: ☆☆☆☆☆	*Substantiality:* ☆☆☆☆☆
Plot: ☆☆☆☆☆	*Impactfulness:* ☆☆☆☆☆

Overall Rating: ☆☆☆☆☆

RECOMMEND? ○ *Yes* ○ *No*

QUOTES/REFLECTIONS/EPIPHANIES:
_____
_____
_____
_____
_____
_____
_____
_____

TITLE:

Author: _____ Publisher: _____

FORMAT: ○ Hardcover ○ Paperback ○ Ebook ○ Audiobook
CATEGORY: ○ Fiction ○ Non-fiction Genre/Subject: _____
SOURCE: ○ Bought ○ Borrowed ○ Received from: _____

Page Count: _____
Date Started: _____
Date Finished: _____

WHY I CHOSE THIS BOOK:
_____
_____

♔ FAVORITE PART:
(draw or describe)

✎ NOTES/REVIEW:

FICTION	NON-FICTION
Ease of Reading:	Ease of Reading:
☆☆☆☆☆	☆☆☆☆☆
Characters:	Substantiality:
☆☆☆☆☆	☆☆☆☆☆
Plot:	Impactfulness:
☆☆☆☆☆	☆☆☆☆☆

Overall Rating: ☆☆☆☆☆

🎖 RECOMMEND? ○ Yes ○ No

💡 QUOTES/REFLECTIONS/EPIPHANIES:
_____
_____
_____
_____
_____
_____
_____

📚 **TITLE:**

Author: _____ *Publisher:* _____

FORMAT: ○ *Hardcover* ○ *Paperback* ○ *Ebook* ○ *Audiobook*
CATEGORY: ○ *Fiction* ○ *Non-fiction* *Genre/Subject:* _____
SOURCE: ○ *Bought* ○ *Borrowed* ○ *Received from:* _____

Page Count: _____
Date Started: _____
Date Finished: _____

📖 *WHY I CHOSE THIS BOOK:*
_____
_____

👑 *FAVORITE PART:*
(draw or describe)

🖋 *NOTES/REVIEW:*
_____
_____
_____
_____
_____
_____
_____
_____
_____
_____
_____
_____
_____
_____
_____
_____
_____

FICTION	NON-FICTION
Ease of Reading:	Ease of Reading:
☆☆☆☆☆	☆☆☆☆☆
Characters:	Substantiality:
☆☆☆☆☆	☆☆☆☆☆
Plot:	Impactfulness:
☆☆☆☆☆	☆☆☆☆☆

Overall Rating: ☆☆☆☆☆

🏅 *RECOMMEND?* ○ *Yes* ○ *No*

💡 *QUOTES/REFLECTIONS/EPIPHANIES:*
_____
_____
_____
_____
_____
_____
_____
_____

TITLE:

Author: _____ Publisher: _____

FORMAT: ○ Hardcover ○ Paperback ○ Ebook ○ Audiobook
CATEGORY: ○ Fiction ○ Non-fiction Genre/Subject: _____
SOURCE: ○ Bought ○ Borrowed ○ Received from: _____

Page Count: _____
Date Started: _____
Date Finished: _____

WHY I CHOSE THIS BOOK:
_____
_____

♛ FAVORITE PART:
(draw or describe)

✎ NOTES/REVIEW:
_____
_____
_____
_____
_____
_____
_____
_____
_____
_____
_____
_____
_____
_____
_____
_____
_____

FICTION	NON-FICTION
Ease of Reading:	Ease of Reading:
☆☆☆☆☆	☆☆☆☆☆
Characters:	Substantiality:
☆☆☆☆☆	☆☆☆☆☆
Plot:	Impactfulness:
☆☆☆☆☆	☆☆☆☆☆

Overall Rating: ☆☆☆☆☆

🎖 RECOMMEND? ○ Yes ○ No

💡 QUOTES/REFLECTIONS/EPIPHANIES:
_____
_____
_____
_____
_____
_____
_____
_____

📚 **TITLE:**

Author: _____ *Publisher:* _____

FORMAT: ○ *Hardcover*   ○ *Paperback*   ○ *Ebook*   ○ *Audiobook*
CATEGORY: ○ *Fiction* ○ *Non-fiction* *Genre/Subject:* _____
SOURCE: ○ *Bought* ○ *Borrowed* ○ *Received from:* _____

Page Count: _____
Date Started: _____
Date Finished: _____

📖 *WHY I CHOSE THIS BOOK:*
_____
_____

👑 *FAVORITE PART:*
(draw or describe)

✒ *NOTES/REVIEW:*
_____
_____
_____
_____
_____
_____
_____
_____
_____
_____
_____
_____
_____
_____
_____
_____

FICTION	NON-FICTION
Ease of Reading: ☆☆☆☆☆	Ease of Reading: ☆☆☆☆☆
Characters: ☆☆☆☆☆	Substantiality: ☆☆☆☆☆
Plot: ☆☆☆☆☆	Impactfulness: ☆☆☆☆☆

Overall Rating: ☆☆☆☆☆

🏅 *RECOMMEND?* ○ *Yes* ○ *No*

💡 *QUOTES/REFLECTIONS/EPIPHANIES:*
_____
_____
_____
_____
_____
_____
_____
_____

📚 **TITLE:**

Author: _____ Publisher: _____

FORMAT: ○ Hardcover ○ Paperback ○ Ebook ○ Audiobook
CATEGORY: ○ Fiction ○ Non-fiction Genre/Subject: _____
SOURCE: ○ Bought ○ Borrowed ○ Received from: _____

Page Count: _____
Date Started: _____
Date Finished: _____

📖 **WHY I CHOSE THIS BOOK:**
_____
_____

👑 **FAVORITE PART:**
(draw or describe)

✒ **NOTES/REVIEW:**
_____
_____
_____
_____
_____
_____
_____
_____
_____
_____
_____
_____
_____
_____
_____
_____
_____

FICTION	NON-FICTION
Ease of Reading:	Ease of Reading:
☆☆☆☆☆	☆☆☆☆☆
Characters:	Substantiality:
☆☆☆☆☆	☆☆☆☆☆
Plot:	Impactfulness:
☆☆☆☆☆	☆☆☆☆☆

Overall Rating: ☆☆☆☆☆

🎖 **RECOMMEND?** ○ Yes ○ No

💡 **QUOTES/REFLECTIONS/EPIPHANIES:**
_____
_____
_____
_____
_____
_____
_____

TITLE:

Author: _____ Publisher: _____

FORMAT: ○ Hardcover ○ Paperback ○ Ebook ○ Audiobook
CATEGORY: ○ Fiction ○ Non-fiction Genre/Subject: _____
SOURCE: ○ Bought ○ Borrowed ○ Received from: _____

Page Count: _____
Date Started: _____
Date Finished: _____

📖 WHY I CHOSE THIS BOOK:
_____
_____

♕ FAVORITE PART:
(draw or describe)

✒ NOTES/REVIEW:
_____
_____
_____
_____
_____
_____
_____
_____
_____
_____
_____
_____
_____
_____
_____
_____

FICTION	NON-FICTION
Ease of Reading: ☆☆☆☆☆	Ease of Reading: ☆☆☆☆☆
Characters: ☆☆☆☆☆	Substantiality: ☆☆☆☆☆
Plot: ☆☆☆☆☆	Impactfulness: ☆☆☆☆☆

Overall Rating: ☆☆☆☆☆

🏵 RECOMMEND? ○ Yes ○ No

💡 QUOTES/REFLECTIONS/EPIPHANIES:
_____
_____
_____
_____
_____
_____
_____
_____

TITLE:

Author: _____ Publisher: _____

FORMAT: ○ Hardcover ○ Paperback ○ Ebook ○ Audiobook
CATEGORY: ○ Fiction ○ Non-fiction Genre/Subject: _____
SOURCE: ○ Bought ○ Borrowed ○ Received from: _____

Page Count: _____
Date Started: _____
Date Finished: _____

WHY I CHOSE THIS BOOK:
_____
_____

♛ FAVORITE PART:
(draw or describe)

✎ NOTES/REVIEW:
_____
_____
_____
_____
_____
_____
_____
_____
_____
_____
_____
_____
_____
_____
_____
_____
_____

FICTION	NON-FICTION
Ease of Reading: ☆☆☆☆☆	Ease of Reading: ☆☆☆☆☆
Characters: ☆☆☆☆☆	Substantiality: ☆☆☆☆☆
Plot: ☆☆☆☆☆	Impactfulness: ☆☆☆☆☆

Overall Rating: ☆☆☆☆☆

🎗 RECOMMEND? ○ Yes ○ No

💡 QUOTES/REFLECTIONS/EPIPHANIES:
_____
_____
_____
_____
_____
_____
_____
_____

TITLE:

Author: _____ *Publisher:* _____

FORMAT: ○ *Hardcover*   ○ *Paperback*   ○ *Ebook*   ○ *Audiobook*
CATEGORY: ○ *Fiction* ○ *Non-fiction* *Genre/Subject:* _____
SOURCE: ○ *Bought* ○ *Borrowed* ○ *Received from:* _____

Page Count: _____
Date Started: _____
Date Finished: _____

WHY I CHOSE THIS BOOK:
_____
_____

FAVORITE PART:
(draw or describe)

NOTES/REVIEW:
_____
_____
_____
_____
_____
_____
_____
_____
_____
_____
_____
_____
_____
_____
_____
_____

FICTION	*NON-FICTION*
Ease of Reading: ☆☆☆☆☆	*Ease of Reading:* ☆☆☆☆☆
Characters: ☆☆☆☆☆	*Substantiality:* ☆☆☆☆☆
Plot: ☆☆☆☆☆	*Impactfulness:* ☆☆☆☆☆

Overall Rating: ☆☆☆☆☆

RECOMMEND? ○ *Yes* ○ *No*

QUOTES/REFLECTIONS/EPIPHANIES:
_____
_____
_____
_____
_____
_____
_____
_____

📚 TITLE:

Author: _____ Publisher: _____

FORMAT: ○ Hardcover   ○ Paperback   ○ Ebook   ○ Audiobook
CATEGORY: ○ Fiction ○ Non-fiction   Genre/Subject: _____
SOURCE: ○ Bought ○ Borrowed ○ Received from: _____

Page Count: _____
Date Started: _____
Date Finished: _____

📖 WHY I CHOSE THIS BOOK:
_____
_____

👑 FAVORITE PART:
(draw or describe)

✒ NOTES/REVIEW:
_____
_____
_____
_____
_____
_____
_____
_____
_____
_____
_____
_____
_____
_____
_____
_____

FICTION	NON-FICTION
Ease of Reading: ☆☆☆☆☆	Ease of Reading: ☆☆☆☆☆
Characters: ☆☆☆☆☆	Substantiality: ☆☆☆☆☆
Plot: ☆☆☆☆☆	Impactfulness: ☆☆☆☆☆

Overall Rating: ☆☆☆☆☆

🎖 RECOMMEND?   ○ Yes   ○ No

💡 QUOTES/REFLECTIONS/EPIPHANIES:
_____
_____
_____
_____
_____
_____
_____
_____

TITLE:

Author: _____ *Publisher:* _____

FORMAT: ○ *Hardcover*   ○ *Paperback*   ○ *Ebook*   ○ *Audiobook*
CATEGORY: ○ *Fiction* ○ *Non-fiction*   *Genre/Subject:* _____
SOURCE: ○ *Bought* ○ *Borrowed* ○ *Received from:* _____

Page Count: _____
Date Started: _____
Date Finished: _____

📖 *WHY I CHOSE THIS BOOK:*
_____
_____

♕ *FAVORITE PART:*
(draw or describe)

✍ *NOTES/REVIEW:*

FICTION	NON-FICTION
Ease of Reading: ☆☆☆☆☆	*Ease of Reading:* ☆☆☆☆☆
Characters: ☆☆☆☆☆	*Substantiality:* ☆☆☆☆☆
Plot: ☆☆☆☆☆	*Impactfulness:* ☆☆☆☆☆

Overall Rating: ☆☆☆☆☆

🎖 *RECOMMEND?* ○ *Yes* ○ *No*

💡 *QUOTES/REFLECTIONS/EPIPHANIES:*
_____
_____
_____
_____
_____
_____
_____
_____

TITLE:

Author: _____ Publisher: _____

FORMAT: ○ Hardcover ○ Paperback ○ Ebook ○ Audiobook
CATEGORY: ○ Fiction ○ Non-fiction Genre/Subject: _____
SOURCE: ○ Bought ○ Borrowed ○ Received from: _____

Page Count: _____
Date Started: _____
Date Finished: _____

WHY I CHOSE THIS BOOK:
_____
_____

♔ FAVORITE PART:
(draw or describe)

✎ NOTES/REVIEW:
_____
_____
_____
_____
_____
_____
_____
_____
_____
_____
_____
_____
_____
_____
_____

FICTION	NON-FICTION
Ease of Reading:	Ease of Reading:
☆☆☆☆☆	☆☆☆☆☆
Characters:	Substantiality:
☆☆☆☆☆	☆☆☆☆☆
Plot:	Impactfulness:
☆☆☆☆☆	☆☆☆☆☆

Overall Rating: ☆☆☆☆☆

⚘ RECOMMEND? ○ Yes ○ No

☀ QUOTES/REFLECTIONS/EPIPHANIES:
_____
_____
_____
_____
_____
_____
_____
_____

TITLE:

Author: _____ Publisher: _____

FORMAT: ○ Hardcover   ○ Paperback   ○ Ebook   ○ Audiobook
CATEGORY: ○ Fiction ○ Non-fiction   Genre/Subject: _____
SOURCE: ○ Bought ○ Borrowed ○ Received from: _____

Page Count: _____
Date Started: _____
Date Finished: _____

WHY I CHOSE THIS BOOK:
_____
_____

FAVORITE PART:
(draw or describe)

NOTES/REVIEW:
_____
_____
_____
_____
_____
_____
_____
_____
_____
_____
_____
_____
_____
_____
_____

FICTION	NON-FICTION
Ease of Reading:	Ease of Reading:
☆☆☆☆☆	☆☆☆☆☆
Characters:	Substantiality:
☆☆☆☆☆	☆☆☆☆☆
Plot:	Impactfulness:
☆☆☆☆☆	☆☆☆☆☆

Overall Rating: ☆☆☆☆☆

RECOMMEND?   ○ Yes   ○ No

QUOTES/REFLECTIONS/EPIPHANIES:
_____
_____
_____
_____
_____
_____
_____
_____
_____

📚 **TITLE:**

Author: _____ *Publisher:* _____

FORMAT: ○ *Hardcover*   ○ *Paperback*   ○ *Ebook*   ○ *Audiobook*
CATEGORY: ○ *Fiction* ○ *Non-fiction*   *Genre/Subject:* _____
SOURCE: ○ *Bought* ○ *Borrowed* ○ *Received from:* _____

Page Count: _____
Date Started: _____
Date Finished: _____

📖 *WHY I CHOSE THIS BOOK:*
_____
_____

👑 *FAVORITE PART:*
(draw or describe)

✒️ *NOTES/REVIEW:*
_____
_____
_____
_____
_____
_____
_____
_____
_____
_____
_____
_____
_____
_____
_____
_____
_____
_____

FICTION	NON-FICTION
Ease of Reading:	Ease of Reading:
☆☆☆☆☆	☆☆☆☆☆
Characters:	Substantiality:
☆☆☆☆☆	☆☆☆☆☆
Plot:	Impactfulness:
☆☆☆☆☆	☆☆☆☆☆

Overall Rating: ☆☆☆☆☆

🏅 *RECOMMEND?*   ○ *Yes*   ○ *No*

💡 *QUOTES/REFLECTIONS/EPIPHANIES:*
_____
_____
_____
_____
_____
_____
_____
_____

📚 **TITLE:**

Author: _____ *Publisher:* _____

FORMAT: ○ *Hardcover* ○ *Paperback* ○ *Ebook* ○ *Audiobook*
CATEGORY: ○ *Fiction* ○ *Non-fiction* *Genre/Subject:* _____
SOURCE: ○ *Bought* ○ *Borrowed* ○ *Received from:* _____

Page Count: _____
Date Started: _____
Date Finished: _____

📖 *WHY I CHOSE THIS BOOK:*
_____
_____

👑 *FAVORITE PART:*
(draw or describe)

🖋 *NOTES/REVIEW:*
_____
_____
_____
_____
_____
_____
_____
_____
_____
_____
_____
_____
_____
_____
_____
_____
_____

FICTION	NON-FICTION
Ease of Reading: ☆☆☆☆☆	Ease of Reading: ☆☆☆☆☆
Characters: ☆☆☆☆☆	Substantiality: ☆☆☆☆☆
Plot: ☆☆☆☆☆	Impactfulness: ☆☆☆☆☆

Overall Rating: ☆☆☆☆☆

🏅 *RECOMMEND?* ○ *Yes* ○ *No*

💡 *QUOTES/REFLECTIONS/EPIPHANIES:*
_____
_____
_____
_____
_____
_____
_____
_____

📚 **TITLE:**

Author: _____ *Publisher:* _____

FORMAT: ○ *Hardcover* ○ *Paperback* ○ *Ebook* ○ *Audiobook*
CATEGORY: ○ *Fiction* ○ *Non-fiction* *Genre/Subject:* _____
SOURCE: ○ *Bought* ○ *Borrowed* ○ *Received from:* _____

Page Count: _____
Date Started: _____
Date Finished: _____

📖 *WHY I CHOSE THIS BOOK:*
_____
_____

👑 *FAVORITE PART:*
(draw or describe)

✒️ *NOTES/REVIEW:*
_____
_____
_____
_____
_____
_____
_____
_____
_____
_____
_____
_____
_____
_____
_____
_____
_____
_____

FICTION	NON-FICTION
Ease of Reading:	Ease of Reading:
☆☆☆☆☆	☆☆☆☆☆
Characters:	Substantiality:
☆☆☆☆☆	☆☆☆☆☆
Plot:	Impactfulness:
☆☆☆☆☆	☆☆☆☆☆

Overall Rating: ☆☆☆☆☆

🎖️ *RECOMMEND?* ○ *Yes* ○ *No*

💡 *QUOTES/REFLECTIONS/EPIPHANIES:*
_____
_____
_____
_____
_____
_____
_____
_____

TITLE:

Author: _____ *Publisher:* _____

FORMAT: ○ *Hardcover* ○ *Paperback* ○ *Ebook* ○ *Audiobook*
CATEGORY: ○ *Fiction* ○ *Non-fiction* *Genre/Subject:* _____
SOURCE: ○ *Bought* ○ *Borrowed* ○ *Received from:* _____

Page Count: _____
Date Started: _____
Date Finished: _____

📖 *WHY I CHOSE THIS BOOK:*
_____
_____

♛ *FAVORITE PART:*
(draw or describe)

✒ *NOTES/REVIEW:*
_____
_____
_____
_____
_____
_____
_____
_____
_____
_____
_____
_____
_____
_____
_____
_____
_____

FICTION	NON-FICTION
Ease of Reading:	Ease of Reading:
☆☆☆☆☆	☆☆☆☆☆
Characters:	Substantiality:
☆☆☆☆☆	☆☆☆☆☆
Plot:	Impactfulness:
☆☆☆☆☆	☆☆☆☆☆
Overall Rating: ☆☆☆☆☆	

🏅 *RECOMMEND?* ○ *Yes* ○ *No*

💡 *QUOTES/REFLECTIONS/EPIPHANIES:*
_____
_____
_____
_____
_____
_____
_____
_____

TITLE:

Author: _____ Publisher: _____

FORMAT: ○ Hardcover ○ Paperback ○ Ebook ○ Audiobook
CATEGORY: ○ Fiction ○ Non-fiction Genre/Subject: _____
SOURCE: ○ Bought ○ Borrowed ○ Received from: _____

Page Count: _____
Date Started: _____
Date Finished: _____

WHY I CHOSE THIS BOOK:
_____
_____

♕ FAVORITE PART:
(draw or describe)

NOTES/REVIEW:
_____
_____
_____
_____
_____
_____
_____
_____
_____
_____
_____
_____
_____
_____
_____
_____
_____

FICTION	NON-FICTION
Ease of Reading: ☆☆☆☆☆	Ease of Reading: ☆☆☆☆☆
Characters: ☆☆☆☆☆	Substantiality: ☆☆☆☆☆
Plot: ☆☆☆☆☆	Impactfulness: ☆☆☆☆☆

Overall Rating: ☆☆☆☆☆

RECOMMEND? ○ Yes ○ No

QUOTES/REFLECTIONS/EPIPHANIES:
_____
_____
_____
_____
_____
_____
_____
_____

TITLE:

Author: _____ Publisher: _____

FORMAT: ○ Hardcover   ○ Paperback   ○ Ebook   ○ Audiobook
CATEGORY: ○ Fiction ○ Non-fiction   Genre/Subject: _____
SOURCE: ○ Bought ○ Borrowed ○ Received from: _____

Page Count: _____
Date Started: _____
Date Finished: _____

📖 WHY I CHOSE THIS BOOK:
_____
_____

👑 FAVORITE PART:
(draw or describe)

✒ NOTES/REVIEW:
_____
_____
_____
_____
_____
_____
_____
_____
_____
_____
_____
_____
_____
_____
_____
_____
_____

FICTION	NON-FICTION
Ease of Reading:	Ease of Reading:
☆☆☆☆☆	☆☆☆☆☆
Characters:	Substantiality:
☆☆☆☆☆	☆☆☆☆☆
Plot:	Impactfulness:
☆☆☆☆☆	☆☆☆☆☆

Overall Rating: ☆☆☆☆☆

🎖 RECOMMEND?   ○ Yes   ○ No

💡 QUOTES/REFLECTIONS/EPIPHANIES:
_____
_____
_____
_____
_____
_____
_____
_____

TITLE:

Author: _____ Publisher: _____

FORMAT: ○ Hardcover   ○ Paperback   ○ Ebook   ○ Audiobook
CATEGORY: ○ Fiction ○ Non-fiction   Genre/Subject: _____
SOURCE: ○ Bought ○ Borrowed ○ Received from: _____

Page Count: _____
Date Started: _____
Date Finished: _____

📖 WHY I CHOSE THIS BOOK:
_____
_____

👑 FAVORITE PART:
(draw or describe)

✒ NOTES/REVIEW:
_____
_____
_____
_____
_____
_____
_____
_____
_____
_____
_____
_____
_____
_____
_____
_____

FICTION	NON-FICTION
Ease of Reading:	Ease of Reading:
☆☆☆☆☆	☆☆☆☆☆
Characters:	Substantiality:
☆☆☆☆☆	☆☆☆☆☆
Plot:	Impactfulness:
☆☆☆☆☆	☆☆☆☆☆

Overall Rating: ☆☆☆☆☆

🎖 RECOMMEND?   ○ Yes   ○ No

💡 QUOTES/REFLECTIONS/EPIPHANIES:
_____
_____
_____
_____
_____
_____
_____
_____

TITLE:

Author: _____ Publisher: _____

FORMAT: ○ Hardcover   ○ Paperback   ○ Ebook   ○ Audiobook
CATEGORY: ○ Fiction ○ Non-fiction Genre/Subject: _____
SOURCE: ○ Bought ○ Borrowed ○ Received from: _____

Page Count: _____
Date Started: _____
Date Finished: _____

📖 WHY I CHOSE THIS BOOK:
_____
_____

👑 FAVORITE PART:
(draw or describe)

✍ NOTES/REVIEW:
_____
_____
_____
_____
_____
_____
_____
_____
_____
_____
_____
_____
_____
_____
_____

FICTION	NON-FICTION
Ease of Reading:	Ease of Reading:
☆☆☆☆☆	☆☆☆☆☆
Characters:	Substantiality:
☆☆☆☆☆	☆☆☆☆☆
Plot:	Impactfulness:
☆☆☆☆☆	☆☆☆☆☆

Overall Rating: ☆☆☆☆☆

🏅 RECOMMEND?   ○ Yes   ○ No

💡 QUOTES/REFLECTIONS/EPIPHANIES:
_____
_____
_____
_____
_____
_____
_____
_____

TITLE:

Author: _____ Publisher: _____

FORMAT: ○ Hardcover ○ Paperback ○ Ebook ○ Audiobook
CATEGORY: ○ Fiction ○ Non-fiction Genre/Subject: _____
SOURCE: ○ Bought ○ Borrowed ○ Received from: _____

Page Count: _____
Date Started: _____
Date Finished: _____

📖 WHY I CHOSE THIS BOOK:
_____
_____

♛ FAVORITE PART:
(draw or describe)

✍ NOTES/REVIEW:

FICTION	NON-FICTION
Ease of Reading:	Ease of Reading:
☆☆☆☆☆	☆☆☆☆☆
Characters:	Substantiality:
☆☆☆☆☆	☆☆☆☆☆
Plot:	Impactfulness:
☆☆☆☆☆	☆☆☆☆☆

Overall Rating: ☆☆☆☆☆

🏅 RECOMMEND? ○ Yes ○ No

💡 QUOTES/REFLECTIONS/EPIPHANIES:
_____
_____
_____
_____
_____
_____

TITLE:

Author: _____ *Publisher:* _____

FORMAT: ○ *Hardcover* ○ *Paperback* ○ *Ebook* ○ *Audiobook*
CATEGORY: ○ *Fiction* ○ *Non-fiction* *Genre/Subject:* _____
SOURCE: ○ *Bought* ○ *Borrowed* ○ *Received from:* _____

Page Count: _____
Date Started: _____
Date Finished: _____

WHY I CHOSE THIS BOOK:

_____

♔ *FAVORITE PART:*
(draw or describe)

✎ *NOTES/REVIEW:*

FICTION	NON-FICTION
Ease of Reading: ☆☆☆☆☆	Ease of Reading: ☆☆☆☆☆
Characters: ☆☆☆☆☆	Substantiality: ☆☆☆☆☆
Plot: ☆☆☆☆☆	Impactfulness: ☆☆☆☆☆
Overall Rating: ☆☆☆☆☆	

🎖 *RECOMMEND?* ○ *Yes* ○ *No*

💡 *QUOTES/REFLECTIONS/EPIPHANIES:*

_____
_____
_____
_____
_____
_____
_____
_____

📚 **TITLE:**

Author: _____ *Publisher:* _____

FORMAT: ○ *Hardcover* ○ *Paperback* ○ *Ebook* ○ *Audiobook*
CATEGORY: ○ *Fiction* ○ *Non-fiction* *Genre/Subject:* _____
SOURCE: ○ *Bought* ○ *Borrowed* ○ *Received from:* _____

Page Count: _____
Date Started: _____
Date Finished: _____

📖 *WHY I CHOSE THIS BOOK:*
_____
_____

👑 *FAVORITE PART:*
(draw or describe)

✒️ *NOTES/REVIEW:*
_____
_____
_____
_____
_____
_____
_____
_____
_____
_____
_____
_____
_____
_____
_____
_____
_____
_____

FICTION	NON-FICTION
Ease of Reading:	Ease of Reading:
☆☆☆☆☆	☆☆☆☆☆
Characters:	Substantiality:
☆☆☆☆☆	☆☆☆☆☆
Plot:	Impactfulness:
☆☆☆☆☆	☆☆☆☆☆

Overall Rating: ☆☆☆☆☆

🎖️ *RECOMMEND?* ○ *Yes* ○ *No*

💡 *QUOTES/REFLECTIONS/EPIPHANIES:*
_____
_____
_____
_____
_____
_____
_____
_____

📚 TITLE:

Author: _____ *Publisher:* _____

FORMAT: ○ *Hardcover*   ○ *Paperback*   ○ *Ebook*   ○ *Audiobook*
CATEGORY: ○ *Fiction* ○ *Non-fiction* *Genre/Subject:* _____
SOURCE: ○ *Bought* ○ *Borrowed* ○ *Received from:* _____

Page Count: _____
Date Started: _____
Date Finished: _____

📖 *WHY I CHOSE THIS BOOK:*
_____
_____

👑 *FAVORITE PART:*
(draw or describe)

✍ *NOTES/REVIEW:*
_____
_____
_____
_____
_____
_____
_____
_____
_____
_____
_____
_____
_____
_____
_____
_____

FICTION	NON-FICTION
Ease of Reading:	Ease of Reading:
☆☆☆☆☆	☆☆☆☆☆
Characters:	Substantiality:
☆☆☆☆☆	☆☆☆☆☆
Plot:	Impactfulness:
☆☆☆☆☆	☆☆☆☆☆

Overall Rating: ☆☆☆☆☆

🏅 *RECOMMEND?* ○ *Yes* ○ *No*

💡 *QUOTES/REFLECTIONS/EPIPHANIES:*
_____
_____
_____
_____
_____
_____
_____
_____

📚 TITLE:

Author: _____ Publisher: _____

FORMAT: ○ Hardcover   ○ Paperback   ○ Ebook   ○ Audiobook
CATEGORY: ○ Fiction ○ Non-fiction   Genre/Subject: _____
SOURCE: ○ Bought   ○ Borrowed   ○ Received from: _____

Page Count: _____
Date Started: _____
Date Finished: _____

📖 WHY I CHOSE THIS BOOK:
_____
_____

👑 FAVORITE PART:
(draw or describe)

✒ NOTES/REVIEW:

FICTION	NON-FICTION
Ease of Reading:	Ease of Reading:
☆☆☆☆☆	☆☆☆☆☆
Characters:	Substantiality:
☆☆☆☆☆	☆☆☆☆☆
Plot:	Impactfulness:
☆☆☆☆☆	☆☆☆☆☆

Overall Rating: ☆☆☆☆☆

🏅 RECOMMEND?   ○ Yes   ○ No

💡 QUOTES/REFLECTIONS/EPIPHANIES:
_____
_____
_____
_____
_____
_____
_____

📚 **TITLE:**

Author: _____ *Publisher:* _____

FORMAT: ○ *Hardcover* ○ *Paperback* ○ *Ebook* ○ *Audiobook*
CATEGORY: ○ *Fiction* ○ *Non-fiction* *Genre/Subject:* _____
SOURCE: ○ *Bought* ○ *Borrowed* ○ *Received from:* _____

Page Count: _____
Date Started: _____
Date Finished: _____

📖 *WHY I CHOSE THIS BOOK:*
_____
_____

👑 *FAVORITE PART:*
(draw or describe)

🖋 *NOTES/REVIEW:*
_____
_____
_____
_____
_____
_____
_____
_____
_____
_____
_____
_____
_____
_____
_____
_____
_____

FICTION	NON-FICTION
Ease of Reading:	Ease of Reading:
☆☆☆☆☆	☆☆☆☆☆
Characters:	Substantiality:
☆☆☆☆☆	☆☆☆☆☆
Plot:	Impactfulness:
☆☆☆☆☆	☆☆☆☆☆

Overall Rating: ☆☆☆☆☆

🏅 *RECOMMEND?* ○ *Yes* ○ *No*

💡 *QUOTES/REFLECTIONS/EPIPHANIES:*
_____
_____
_____
_____
_____
_____
_____
_____

TITLE:

Author: _____ Publisher: _____

FORMAT: ○ Hardcover ○ Paperback ○ Ebook ○ Audiobook
CATEGORY: ○ Fiction ○ Non-fiction Genre/Subject: _____
SOURCE: ○ Bought ○ Borrowed ○ Received from: _____

Page Count: _____
Date Started: _____
Date Finished: _____

WHY I CHOSE THIS BOOK:
_____
_____

♕ FAVORITE PART:
(draw or describe)

✎ NOTES/REVIEW:

FICTION	NON-FICTION
Ease of Reading:	Ease of Reading:
☆☆☆☆☆	☆☆☆☆☆
Characters:	Substantiality:
☆☆☆☆☆	☆☆☆☆☆
Plot:	Impactfulness:
☆☆☆☆☆	☆☆☆☆☆

Overall Rating: ☆☆☆☆☆

🎗 RECOMMEND? ○ Yes ○ No

💡 QUOTES/REFLECTIONS/EPIPHANIES:
_____
_____
_____
_____
_____
_____
_____

Printed in Great Britain
by Amazon